On Inception

On Inception

Martin Heidegger

Translated by Peter Hanly

INDIANA UNIVERSITY PRESS

This book is a publication of

Indiana University Press
Office of Scholarly Publishing
Herman B Wells Library 350
1320 East 10th Street
Bloomington, Indiana 47405 USA

iupress.org

Published in German as Martin Heidegger *Gesamtausgabe 70: Über den Anfang*
© Vittorio Klostermann GmbH, Frankfurt am Main, 2005.
English translation © 2023 by Indiana University Press

Manufactured in the United States of America

First printing 2023

Cataloging information is available from the Library of Congress.

ISBN 978-0-253-06684-8 (hardback)
ISBN 978-0-253-06685-5 (ebook)

Contents

The Differentiation and the Difference

The Inception as Receding

**II. INCEPTION AND INCEPTIVE THINKING
THE CREATIVE THINKING OF INCEPTION**

III. EVENT AND BEING-THERE
A. The Event

B. Event and Dis-appropriation

C. Being-there
(Disposition - Attunement)
Human - Gods

Preface

The sought-after word of *inception* can always only keep the appearance of being a presentation and must often sound, contrary to its aim, like a report.

That is why the appropriate title for such an attempt is just the heading:

On Inception

This title contains within it the semblance that thinking might already be "beyond" inception, whereas this is never possible and never to be attempted.

Sometime coming
Undertaken from beyng
They risk
The saying
Of the truth of beyng:
Event of inception
Toward issuance in the parting

Learn to thank
And you might think

*

It is not in vain
All is singular

*

Beyng—a result of thinking?
Thinking is already evental appropriation of beyng

I. The Incipience of Inception

1. What Does "Inception" Say?

Nothing can be twisted out from some clutched-at definition. And even if this were possible, that "word" would still not be that which should here say the essential. Here, the word is the telling of the truth of beyng. And so, it is the thinking of beyng that must say and must justify, that must even demand the word, in as much as it is beyng itself that beckons back toward this "essence" that is to be called inception, whose essential unfolding and essentiality is determined in that essence.

The thinking of beyng as inception thinks toward the essence of beyng as event. Both essential occurrences [*Wesungen*]—appropriative event and inception—belong together. Through this thinking, "beyng" as essential word is not erased; it does, though, lose that exclusive primacy that, especially in the form of the essential imprint of metaphysics ("beingness"), denied every essential questioning of beyng itself, by making it seem as if every determining of being might be contained within the form of a question about the beingness of being (the question within which all "ontology" plays out).

If it is "inception" that says the truth of beyng, then how is it that we know of being? In the first place, through recollecting that we know and understand being, though without, to be sure, taking any special "notice" of this understanding. The understanding of "being" is essentially far removed from a knowing of beyng. That understanding always tends to explain being from out of beings, whereas the knowing of beyng can only be prepared for in a leap beyond the understanding of being and, even then, is not arrived at directly. The creative thinking of beyng in its essence remains what is most difficult for the human being and for the very reasons that suggest that the opposite is the case. It is only from the far distance that thinking enters into this singular essential realm of the most singular: the truth of beyng as event and inception. This is because the essence of the human—still all too concealed—is suspended in and vibrates in the relation of beyng to the human.

The word inception means first of all something like "start": a special position and phase in the sequence of a progression.

But if the word "inception" is, here, to name the essence of beyng and the essentiality of the essence; if, at the same time, beyng cannot be derived from beings; and if beyng is nevertheless not the absolute and unconditioned (something that can be claimed only of beings), then "inception" must name that which unfolds in itself and which, out of that very same essential unfolding, refuses to consider what unfolds as an unconditioned thing-in-itself. Beyng, and its essence as inception (appropriative event), unfolds (incepts, eventuates appropriatively) outside the domain of the absolute and the relative, and of their differentiation.

The thinking that thinks toward this outside is thinking proper and is the only "real" leap.

"Inception" is therefore not the inception of something else; rather, what this word thinks, here, is the taking-in-itself and intercepting of that which is appropriated in the sufficiency of taking-in-itself [an-sich-nehmendes Aus-langen]: the clearing of the openness, the unconcealment. The taking-in-itself is at once unconcealment and concealment.

Inception is the appropriative singularizing [Er-einigung] of this oneness. Inception is, incipiently, the taking-in-itself of concealment, that is, of parting (cf. the parting). In-ception [An-fang] is appropriative event. The in-cepting is the taking hold of and inter-cepting [Sichfangen und Sichauf-fangen] of the event itself, which unfolds as the clearing, veiled by the veil of the nothing.

In-ception [An-fang] is the inter-cepting of itself [Sich-auf-fangen] in the egress to the abyssal ground.

The essence of unconcealment, within which, as sheltering and veiling, concealment lies, has its distinctive mark in letting beings arise into themselves. Thus, it does include beings as such; as this including, this essence is a ground, in the way that we speak of fore-, mid-, and background in a "spatial" sense.

In the simplicity of a unique projection, the essence of beyng as inception thus casts itself toward the knowledge that:

The in-ception is the taking-in-itself of the parting into the abyss.

This taking-in-itself is inceptive appropriation and is thus the appropriative event of incipience.

In-ception is, inceptively (and this means abyssally), the appropriative event.

In the inceptively appropriative event, inception itself is intercepted over its abyss, thus allowing this latter to plunge into its depth as abyssal ground and to rise up to its heights.   ,

But the inceptively appropriative event has its complete essence only in that it clears the inceptive clearing, sustaining the appropriation, and thus eventuates the openness. Such an appropriative eventuation is the inter-vening of the clearing as time-space. This eventuation assigns the in-between (as in-the-midst-of and as meanwhile) to the nothing-less, until the time-span, unfolding out of the appropriation, in which it then arises as a being.

But this inclusive and protective grounding unfolds only in such a way that the ground itself is no longer ground, and essentially and always turns away from what is ground-like, thereby remaining abyssal ground. Concealment, in which unconcealment unfolds, is the egress into the abyssal ground.

The in-cepting incepts inception ever more inceptively [das An-fangen fängt den Anfang je anfänglicher an].

This "increase" is not like that of beings, with degrees, steps, and sequences. It is incipient, and is therefore always singular, discontinuous; one incepting opens up over against another.

The self-inter-cepting in the fissuring of the abyss unfolds in the event.

Beyng, as inception and as event, has that unique essence that enables one to say that "beyng is." Beings only ever arise into being; a being never is but "is" always only a being.

Beings *are* not so long as in this "are" the matter ends (the matter that, here, ought to begin). A being *is* only as a being, and this says: a being, at a certain time, arrives at being but is not itself being.

Beings remain so decisively differentiated from, through, and over against beyng that not even the nothing remains to them as their own; for only beyng unfolds essentially as nothing.

Beings are the nothing-less.

Inception can never be found in beings.

Inception does not determine its essence from progressing; rather, progressing is a possibility of inception. It is from progressing that inception appears in a facile sense as a mere "start." But inception does also unfold in the advancing-away. This latter *is* only inceptively. And in this alone consists its history.

The inception is ever inception. The singularity is fissured into inceptions and only thus arrives at the simplicity of incipience. The talk of multiple inceptions is correct, although it comes from the outside. But it becomes untrue if inceptions come to be reckoned historiographically. To think inceptively—to think in the direction of incipience—is thinking proper, if *thinking* here means the steadfastness of the projection of beyng projected from the casting that vibrates in all eventuation.

We intimate inception in recollecting the truth of beyng and name this recollected inception the "first inception." We intimate incipience and, accordingly, think ahead into the inceptuality of inception, intimating thus the "other inception." It shall be called "other," not in order to lapse into counting, but equally not in order to allocate the number one to the first. The first is the "initial," that from which all essential unfolding of beyng emerges. The initial inception is "once"; it is at the same time "one-time" and unique. And therefore, keeping to itself, [it is] the issuance [*Austragsamkeit*] of the clearing, in the sustainment [*Austragung*] of which the inception takes the parting to itself.

Sufficiency holds the parting, sustaining its essential taking-in-itself. Inception sustains its incipience and thus brings all that is decidable into the simplicity of one decision (either beings or beyng). Inception is sustaining.

That which belongs to inception is therefore sustained and ripe. Only the inceptive is ripe.

2. The Incipience of Inception

(F.I.) In-ception—taking hold of its own abyssal ground into the arrival of the emerging conjoinment.

(O.I.) Inception—taking hold of its own abyssal ground in receding toward the parting.

(F.I.) The taking hold as the gathering and intercepting of unconcealment.

(O.I.) The taking hold as the gathering of the forgetfulness of being into the appropriative event.

The taking hold over the abyssal ground is in each case a distinct abyssal grounding, and this is a concealing as the sheltering and veiling of openness.

In the first inception, the abyssal ground is what is ungrounded in the truth of beyng.

In the other inception, the abyssal ground is what is eventuated in the receding.

Taking hold of itself over the abyssal ground—therefore unconcealment
therefore appropriative eventuation
(Here the difference from "starting" and so on is most easily seen.)

The incipience of the inceptions is the way in which they incept, a way whose scope and configuration is in inception's being in itself the essence of history; for truth essences as inception, and as the sustaining of its specific essence.

Incipience is in each case, in every inception, singular. There is no rule and no law of inception, in the sense of something holding sway "over" inception.

Incipience determines and "is" the essential unfolding of inception.

The incipience of the other inception is determined from out of the appropriative event.

The greater incipience of the first inception
is not that of something earlier but rather later.

Relationships in the inceptive cannot be reckoned-up according to the measure of beings.

And that is also why the essence of history can never be determined from the historiographical, that is, from historiographical apprehending and experiencing.

3. *The Remoteness of Inception*

We can say that heavenly bodies follow their courses and "are," even if no one anywhere, or in any way, represents them. We say this. But *if* we say this, then we must also concede that when there is no representing, "then" there is also no "then" and no "when."

And so, everything is set up by the human and unfolds at its behest.

This could be swiftly foreclosed on, were this ever a domain of "conclusions" and "deductions."

A being is not without being.

Being does not essence without the appropriative event of being-there.

Being-there *is* not without the steadfastness of the human.

But how, then, should beyng remain independent of the human? Just because the human belongs to the grounding of the truth of beyng, this does not mean that beyng depends on the human in such a way that beyng would be established by the human.

So how does the human belong to beyng?

As steadfastness in the clearing, which intercepts the happen-stance of beyng in its truth and safeguards the possibility that a world be configured.

In the whole domain of this preceding question, being is immediately understood as what is constant. Being itself is not being thought in its inceptuality. Thus, one places "value" on the inner certainty of beings in their constancy, as if it was through constant duration that they were most in being [*am seiendsten*].

What is forgotten, though, is to ask with what right this claim about beings might be made, and on what grounds being might be equated with constancy.

What remains entirely beyond reach is the admittedly disconcerting possibility that being, and not just beings, sometimes is not; and that, if decided in this way, the essence of this not-being is such that it even refuses the essential unfolding of the nothing. Thus, being must indeed be entirely remote [*abgeschieden*] in its essence: there can be no destruction or elimination of being, since it is neither produced nor made.

But is remoteness not also, then, still a mode in which beyng is? Certainly. But this remoteness is always egress into the uniqueness of the abyss. Uniqueness knows no continuity. It is in each case inceptive and is every time its own, singular fissuring. The "remaining" that pertains to inception is not a continuing but is rather remoteness as the receding into concealment. Therefore inception, from out of remoteness, is always an abyss of donation, because it guarantees the essence of a giving that, without the nothing, could never be given over.

Beyng, as the abyss of donation, attunes the steadfastness of being-there into the inceptive fundamental attunement of thinking.

Beyng, and only beyng, is. But sometimes beyng is in that it itself allows the clearing as time-space to emerge as the appropriative event of the in-between. There is no "time" that would precede and follow on from beyng and that could serve as a way of ordering. The timeless is not the eternal but is rather the partedness [*Abgeschiedenheit*] of inception into concealment. This is the refusal of the word.

The abruptness of inception and of the event corresponds to the fissuring of the parting [*Abschied*] into the singularity of concealment.

Technical and historiographical calculus (which are of the same essence) have robbed us of every capacity to think time, as time-space, from out of the truth of beyng, and truth itself as the event of inception.

Because beyng is and because only beyng is (beyng, that is, of the essence of evental inception), beyng must therefore also not be. As long as it is not, it is neither time, nor yet the nothing, because the nothing unfolds in beyng and time is the essential unfolding of its truth. Therefore, no period of time can be measured in which beyng escapes into remoteness. The not-being of beyng cannot be determined historiographically but must rather be thought as an essential decisive separation [*Wesensentscheid*], refusing determination. But this only increases what is disconcerting in the abruptness of beyng, which likes to hide in the continuity of beings. Abruptness is the fundamental trait of the time of pro-jecting in which beyng appropriates the human. The technical and historiographical present initially insurmountable obstacles to awakening the knowledge of beyng as inception.

Beyng is inception.

Incipience is the taking and holding-to-itself of the entrance into the abyss and the taking hold that hovers in the in-between.

Incepting is the concealment into the parting.

This concealment is the inceptive, essential unfolding of truth.

Truth is the appropriative eventuation of being-there.

Appropriative eventuation belongs to the appropriative event.

The appropriative event is the incipience of inception, in as much as this incipience, as the inceptively nothing-less, detaches itself over against beings, and in such an "against" lets beings stand forth into the there. The event is beyng.

4. *"Inception" and "Event"*

When beyng is "inception" and "event," and if this saying must likewise let what is said here—its "is"—be determined from inception and event, then this saying immediately issues in a great difficulty.

"Inception," "event" are names of movement and of "becoming." One could try to bring all saying about beyng back around to "that which was uttered long-ago," according at any rate to the view articulated by the historians of the proposition: "being is becoming." This misunderstanding of onto-historical thinking must now be put to rest. Even were it to be in the right (and precisely then), there would arise the difficulty that it now becomes necessary to think through. Beyng is determined here, entirely, only as "formal" and "empty," which means it is not determined at all. Because everywhere the question comes up: "what" is it that begins here? "What" is eventuated?

Is there, then, an "inception" and an event that begins "nothing" and eventuates nothing?

This apparently justified question slips back unawares into metaphysics; or better said: it still comes from there. It initially "thinks" a being and demands of being that it be the beingness of this being, and hence something initiated by an inception or eventuated by an event. Once again, "thinking" sees itself placed before beings as an obstacle and expected to abstract from the beingness of these beings.

But in truth, event is not the empty form of the universal for the sundry eventuations that beings are to be. Event is not an "occurrence" that instantly perishes in its occurring, surfacing and vanishing like a phase in a process, in which case it is the process that would be primary.

The event is in itself its own essential plenitude. It eventuates appropriatively, bringing the clearing of the in-between (amid and in the meantime), that is, of time-space, into the proper domain of inception. The there eventuates the event appropriatively. The eventuated "there" happens as event, that is, belongs to the event and is, therefore, being-there. "Being" "is."

But the appropriative event, in which the proper domain is eventuated—and with it the whole abundance of beyng—is essentially more abundant than any conceivable plenitude of incidents. The question of what, here, might "be eventuated" in the event, already falls short of its essence, in as much as a particular this or that, or any being at all, be it finite or infinite, is what is asked about; all of this remains infinitely different from the appropriative event itself in which, alone, any being can first arise out of itself toward its being.

The simplicity of the appropriative event does not permit its being thought otherwise than from out of itself, its essence thought inceptively every time.

The event is the differentiation of the appropriative event over against that which can arise into manifestation in what is eventuated—over against beings.

But this separative differentiation happens eventually as inception.

And inception is not the inception of something other than what it itself is; equally, inception is not the inception of itself, as if what were being thought of were a producing and causing.

Just as essentially as event, inception is the essential plenitude of its own simpleness.

Inception is the taking-into-itself of the parting.

Inception is concealment, whose unconcealment must be what is primary—emergence amid the still more complete veiling of the essence of being-there.

Inception and event are in a simplicity of essence with unconcealment and concealment, and that means with truth.

The "truth" is of beyng.

Only in advancing away from the inception toward metaphysics does "truth" then become "in intellectu" and "in re," at the same time "logical" and "ontological." But in this way, the essence of truth is not inceptive.

On the other hand, truth is not the "generalizing" of truths; it is itself the first and unique truth.

We are capable of thinking the keenness of the simplicity of the oneness of beyng in its essence as event and inception only when we really "think," which means: when we can risk the leap into the nothing because we are, in our essence, eventuated appropriatively by beyng itself.

5. Beyng?

The first clarity on the long journey of the "question of being" has been achieved. The knowledge, in which this questionability resides, holds that "beyng" is essentially no longer what is to be inceptively inquired after.

Not that the question could be replaced; nor that the question of being should be broken apart. Being remains, always, what is said; however, the essence of beyng is not beyng, but is rather the incepting inception. From this, and as this, beyng incepts (and that means also recedes) into its proper domain. Here, what is intercepted—and what incepts in such self-intercepting—is that which all hasty opinionating about being looks for when, searching for clues in beings, it names the "in-itself" (the "thing-in-itself," and everything that can be covered by this designation).

Beyng, that intercepts itself, and recedes into its "essence" as inception.

But inception, here, is the incepting inception that recedes into itself, not the first emergence and progressing: the ἀρχή. The incepting inception is appropriative event, the receding into the parting. In the circumspection of preparatory inceptive thinking, though, the incepting inception can at first only be named the "other" inception.

The thinking of the other inception is the twisting-free of beyng. The "twisting-free" named here can only be conceived from the incipience of inception; thence, it can step back into itself, begin over [*überfangen*] and let beyng unfold in the parting.

The *twisting-free* is the granting of beyng (and not primarily beings), but a granting that does not just emerge into beyng and toward beyng; rather, in order that it can remain a granting, it is a receding into the parting.

Twisting-free signifies how inception as appropriative event is decided [*entschieden*] in the destitution of the parting [*Abschied*], a destitution that is indeed no lack but rather the uniqueness of the singular.

Twisted-free by inception, beyng does not unfold as deficiency or lack, far rather as the "essence" that inception itself incepts and has incepted.

The essence of *twisting-free* is to be clarified only from the *parting*-character of incipience, meaning that it is revealed only in the other inception.

(But the "twisting-free" can at the same time be a help in surmising something of the essence of the first inception where, for sure, other relations hold sway [cf. Anaximander interpretation].)[1]

*The Twisting-Free of Beyng and the Overcoming of the
Truth of Beings (i.e., of Metaphysics)*

The overcoming of the truth of beings is only a phase (a transition) in the history of beyng, which begins with the twisting-free of beyng, long-concealed at first, in accord with the essence of inception—the event of receding into the parting.

The innermost relationship between overcoming and twisting-free is grounded in the essential relation with differentiation, as the differing toward parting.

---

1. Lecture course, *Grundbegriffe*, summer semester 1941 (GA 51), edited by Petra Jaeger (Frankfurt am Main: Vittorio Klostermann, 1991), 94–123, translated as *Basic Concepts* by Gary Aylesworth (Bloomington: Indiana University Press, 1993).

In metaphysics, the differentiation that underlies the truth of beings is un-recognized; it configures metaphysics into its ownmost structure and is there-fore, for metaphysics, both incomprehensible and indifferent.

In the other inception, by contrast, the parting steps into the clearing of essential concealment, in which it becomes the attuning for the attunement of being-there.

In metaphysics, beings place themselves ahead of being and pass for being itself.

In the other inception, beyng actually steps back into its inceptuality, specifi-cally illuminated as itself (event).

6. Beyng? The Event of Inception as the Receding into Parting

Only in the overcoming of beyng itself does the overcoming of metaphysics even-tuate. Because it is only in the overcoming of beyng that the ground of the pos-sible beginning of metaphysics is left behind. "Parmenides" is the transition from beyng, a transition that, however, only as ἀλήθεια prepares the emergence into metaphysics (being as οὐσια and οὐσια as ἰδέα).

In the first inception the ἀρχή emerges, but incipience begins only in the intimacy of retreat. But the ἀρχή (inception as the disposition of the safekeeping of limits and unconcealment) unfolds in the direction of an advancing away from inception. Incipience begins as receding. In incipience beyng has receded into the safekeeping of the parting.

In the knowledge of beyng as event, beyng is already twisted-free but is not erased. And it should not be erased. And yet difference intercepts beyng in the incipience of receding and parting.

Thus, in crossing into the other inception, beyng long remains what is still said. And yet the step toward the twisting-free, even of beyng, must be risked sometime. Only then does the word become true: πάντα γὰρ τολμητέον—everything is to be risked, that is, not only beings in their entirety, not only be-ingness, not only being, but even beyng.

But the risk is the preparedness for the twisting-free of beyng. Twisting-free is more inceptive than all overcoming—more inceptive, too, than every "sublation." For twisting-free is at the same time the original unfolding [*Er-Wesung*] of beyng itself in inceptedness.

In the twisting-free of beyng toward the incipience of the parting, beyng is both said and questioned, and it is thus that the holding-silent of its twisting-free into inception can take place.

The twisting-free of beyng includes the warrant for the more proper (i.e., more inceptive) question-worthiness of beyng. The twisting-free is not the devaluing of beyng but rather its ultimate acknowledgment.

The twisting-free of beyng, itself an onto-historical event, is hardly to be confused with the apparent doing away with "being" by proclaiming "becoming." Quite apart from [the fact] that this doing away with "being" is just a step of modern metaphysics, the doing away also only seems to be this supposed overcoming. In truth, what is accomplished here is the imprisoning of being, expelled into the unquestionable. The replacing of being by "becoming" (= life = will to power) is not only no overcoming of being, let alone a twisting-free of beyng. This replacing is merely the entanglement in beings, an entanglement that mistakes and at the same time betrays itself, in that it must necessarily set up "being" in the sense of the ensuring in constancy of "life."

By contrast, the twisting-free of beyng encloses in itself the entrance into the intimacy of its essence as inception.

The twisting-free of beyng needs the pure telling of beyng itself. But the twisting-free is at the same time the safekeeping of beyng into the receding of parting.

This is why, in the telling of beyng, what is specifically said is not beyng but rather the event of inception, which can no longer be addressed as beyng.

The first-inceptive question of being asks about the being of beings, yet without ossifying into the question of "*what*" beings might be. In the manner of the first inception, being and only being is asked about, but at the same time, beings are what are named and thought. But the differentiation means nothing. Being is inquired after only in order to name itself, but here it is not initially being that is said but rather, and almost unwittingly, ἀλήθεια and then φύσις.

Since Plato, the question of being asks decisively what beings might be. The question of being itself, resounding in the first inception but not developed, is given up or, better said, is not known and so is admitted into no thoughtful reflection.

Now the question is about the essence of beings and about "essentiality," which is then, once again, located in a highest being. But if what is inquired into is the question of the essence of beyng, then what immediately reveals itself is how beyng recovers its proper truth and that this truth is itself determined as beyng. The beyng of beyng is, then, just the name for the inceptuality of inception, from out of which the twisting-free of beyng into the parting becomes necessary.

For all of us, coming from the metaphysical tradition and locked into its calculus, beyng is already difficult enough, indeed barely thinkable. For beyng demands the rejection of the support of every kind of analogy. The hasty resort, which wants beyng to explain or clarify itself from something else, is the real going astray. For this other of beyng is always only beings. Besides, beyng brooks no shifting into analogy, for it—and it alone—is the claim and the word and the attuning itself.

Beyng itself can alone be named, *it* itself is the telling. And the difficulty, for the chattering human, is to find enough in an essential word for steadfastness in the inceptive.

Nor is beyng that which makes everything possible, insofar as, in the making-possible, what is immediately thought is the reference to actuality and to actualizing; beyng is not the unconditioned, but neither is it the conditioned. Beyng is not the highest, nor the lowest; being is just beyng, and this says: inception.

But now, more difficult still than the subservience to beyng itself and the renunciation of equivalence to beings, is the twisting-free of beyng even into the incipience of inception.

What this twisting-free demands is a disposition that remains, simply, decided on the singularity of inception. And it is precisely this destitution in disposition that will be most difficult for the calculative-metaphysical essence to enter into, insofar as this destitution holds within it the unceasing richness of the inceptive that allows us to await its incipience—waiting, though, not for the arrival of a being but for the distance of the parting. The waiting, and the keeping watch, are no non-possession or wanting-only-to-possess, or indeed any "possessing" at all; rather, they are the attunedness to the attuned voice of the attuning itself, the belonging to the incepting, the acknowledgment of the dignity in which all happens as inception, the not-needing of "power" and, thus, the leave-taking from all the beingness of beings.

7. The Parting

The essence of beyng is inception. The incipience of inception is the parting. Incipience is the event of receding. Receding is the intimacy of incipience. The parting is the still distant arrival of the concealing of the safeguarding in inception of the advancing-away.

The parting is arrival, not into the presencing of something at hand, but rather inceptive arrival, which withdraws into itself, holding within it its most distant distance.

The essence of unconcealment and event are here to be thought together, in order to think always in the inceptive, without slipping away into "sequential" representation.

Parting also does not mean, here, loss and renunciation, nor does it signify a relationship between beings or something experienced from out of them.

Only at home with beyng are we capable of knowing something of the incipience of inception and of thinking the parting.

The receding into the parting appears completely negative if we think metaphysically. But if we inquire after beyng onto-historically, it is inception.

The event of inception is the receding.

The receding is the parting.

The parting is the intimacy of the inceptive appropriating which—in the parting—is pure poetizing, a poetizing that remains inceptive before all the poetry of the "poet" and the modes of thought of the "thinker."

The parting is the concealment of the inception into the intimacy of its event-like incipience.

The overcoming of metaphysics (the truth of beings) is the onto-historical prelude to the twisting-free of beyng itself.

The receding of beyng into the incipience of the parting.

The event of inception is the receding into the parting.

Receding and parting are not "*negativa*" but the incipience of the intimacy of inception.

In the telling that says the event of inception in its onto-historical provenance, the "co-responding" [*Ent-sprechung*] holds sway.

Language stems from the parting.

Language answers to the inception.

The co-responding is twofold.

And because, here, the telling is of the parting, it must therefore be spoken from the proximity and closeness of the most ordinary possessing.

Being in the possession of the "differentiation."

The differentiation—the parting.

The parting is the receding of unconcealment beneath the shelter of the dignity that, as the intimacy of the safeguarding arrival, remains behind in inceptive distance and keeps open the inception in its uniqueness.

The inceptive incipience of inception first begins in the parting. Here it is not a matter of effect, nor of cause.

The parting assigns to each what is proper to it and abandons them in this, thus vouchsafing the arising of beings from themselves.

All arising-forth of beings toward beings is appropriative event.

Parting is not end and cessation, but it is the ultimacy of inception, through which it withdraws into itself, intercepting incipience in itself, purely in order to begin and this alone.

The "ultimacy" of inception is only the inceptuality of its firstness, that is, concealment. Concealment itself begins in the parting; and only now can unconcealment be a bestowal, one whose gift never diminishes the abundance of the singular.

In the parting, the inception intercepts itself in its dignity, resounding into the singularity of the stillness, which nor time nor eternity could possibly measure, as the singularity brooks no measurement and needs no duration to ensure its continuance.

However, if it is explained and reckoned from out of beings, the receding essence of beyng, preserving its inceptive dignity in the parting, is utterly meaningless. If metaphysics and worldview were able to pull themselves together to declare beyng to be the meaningless, then they might yet reach whatever vicinity of beyng their forgetfulness of being permits. This distortion of beyng can, of course, never encounter beyng itself.

All metaphysics is unsuited to the parting, that is, it is incapable of inception.

8. Inception and Veiling and Event

The veiling of inception consists in its calling the parting to itself in incipient seizing [*An-fangen*], stopping it in advance, but in such a way that it emerges as emergence and veils concealment in the acknowledgment of the preeminence of unconcealment. The veiling of inception belongs to incipience.

The veiling gives a hint as to the inceptive essence of the differentiation of beyng and beings.

The veiling is the innermost concealment.

The nothing belongs, also, to the veiled essence of beyng. The nothing, as the in-between granted in the differentiation, belongs to inception. For this is appropriative event, and appropriative event is the inter-vening of the in-between.

9. Inception and Uprising

As the inter-vening of the in-between, the appropriative event is the calling-forth of the nothing-less into being, in order that it be a being. Beings thus rise up into themselves. In that they are given over to being, beings appropriate being in such a way that they henceforth present themselves as that which bears and brings forth being and thereby become the measure and foundation for the determination of being, which is thus configured as beingness. Beings thus rise up (as appropriative event) over against being. This uprising happens from out of inception and belongs to it in such a way that inception risks, in this uprising, the burying of the truth of beyng. This danger is keenest in that it disguises itself by making it appear that only in this way would being be made worthy. Metaphysics is preoccupied with this appearance.

10. Beyng as Staying

As soon as being unconcealed itself as presencing, its essence was mistaken for constancy.

And since, at about the same time, non-being appeared as its alternative, being had to be understood as what stays. The theological-causal interpretation of beings did the rest, establishing the eternal as what is proper to beings.

Whether one places being after becoming or whether one gives the latter precedence, it is in any case the staying that is henceforth the determining mark.

But the essence of staying is equivocal; in presencing, there is already an ambiguity as to whether it should be taken transitionally, as emergence toward egress, or whether, as what has arrived [*Angekommenheit*], it is rigidified into the constancy of what is present. If presencing is determined inceptively from emergence, then the staying cannot be grounded in the first inception, because that inception still covers over its incipience. However, if the incipience of inception is thought as the essential ground of the staying, then the staying becomes the not-letting-go of inceptuality, and is thus not determined by duration and continuity. On the contrary: its distinguishing mark is precisely the *not*-advancing-away from inception, and its unique intimacy with inception's rareness. In this way, "the staying" is thought historically, and against every metaphysical habit.

How far Hölderlin intended this onto-historical staying in his foundational word, or to what extent he was still thinking of and looking for a metaphysically-conceived constancy, can barely be decided.

With the twisting-free of beyng, "staying," as an essential trait of beyng, becomes less important. But it would be quite wrong to think, from this, that one should take it that now only the inconstant "stays"; because this, too, belongs—as essential opposition—to the staying, and remains outside the inceptive.

But beyond this "staying," the inceptive essence of staying must still be creatively returned to in thought.

The metaphysical essence of staying is determined out of presencing. This already veils emergence and unconcealment, and thus also the incipience of inception.

The inceptive essence of staying consists in the regress into inception, in the parting. This is the innermost not-advancing-away from the inception, because the parting has let go of every occasion of advancing-away.

Only the steadfastness of being-there corresponds to this inceptive staying.

The inceptive staying is inception itself, as the calling-to-itself of the parting.

Here, every sense of "duration" loses its import.

11. *The Inexplicability of Beyng*

To acknowledge this means knowing inception and the parting. Incipience is the ground of the poetic-character of beyng.

The parting is the ground for the effective lack of need [*Wirkungsunbedürftigkeit*] that beyng has in respect of beings.

This inceptive-separative [*anfänglich-abschiedliche*] essence of beyng, which returns "essence" itself to essentiality as inception and parting, remains inaccessible to all metaphysics. As will to power, beingness, whose essence still lurks hidden in machination, is separated from beyng as by an abyss.

Beyng is never to be intimated from will to power, nor from any determination of being as actuality; much less is it known that beyng enters into the twisting-free in order to find shelter in the intimacy of inception.

The inceptive essence of beyng brings the question of the relation of beyng to humanity and to divinity into an entirely other domain.

12. The Event of Inception and the Site of the Essence of the Human

The *site* of the *essence* of the human is the where that is allocated to this essence once it has been appropriatively assigned, insofar as this essence has been determined through the relation to being.

The assigning is the allocation into the inception as inception.

The site—the where—is *being-there*.

As being, being-there is itself evental, and not a "being" into which beyng just enters. Being-there belongs to beyng, but beyng never is by the grace of being-there, just as little as being-there is by the grace of any kind of humanity.

13. Being and the Historically Human

The historically human is that which stands in a truth of beings and, albeit unknowingly, lays claim to the truth of being.

Being marks out the human being as historical.

Being lays claim, in the manner of evental happen-stance, to the inter-vening of the human, indeed necessarily so. Nonetheless beyng does not become dependent on the human, nor is it a construction of the human, in the sense of belonging to the objectivity of human representing.

It is in beyng that the claim upon the human as shepherd of the truth of being unfolds.

Being is essential word—as appropriative event, that is, as inception.

Being is inception and has its essence in incipience.

Beyng in no way becomes anthropomorphic through this essential relation of being to the historically human, because this relation is not at all a matter of the human, somehow taken in itself as producing being. Far rather, the essence of the human is determined by being itself as belonging to it; one might indeed see in this a dependency of being on the "human," inasmuch as beyng needs the human—but it needs the human only as a historical being, and as such, he *is* only the happenstance of beyng.

Every reckoning up of dependencies that has already tacitly assumed an objectively present "human" and a "being in itself," preferring now one, now the other to the disadvantage of the former; every dialectical back and forth in a sphere of representability that is not more broadly grounded, or that is taken for "certain": none of this has any purchase here. Here, everything must be separated from whatever pertains to a metaphysical way of thinking, and must be thought from out of the inceptive. And this, always and again, requires the refusal of obvious information for explaining with the aid of derivatives of the inceptive.

In the event of inception the essence of the human as *animal rationale* perishes. Only being-there is inceptive. But *being*-there also remains just the *onto*-historical aftermath of the incipience of inception as receding.

The domain of the human and the divine are inceptively, in essence and in essential claim, shaken.

Inasmuch as, in the receding, the human is still remembered at all, it remains abyssally separated from every sort of preoccupation with the human in any of the various "humanistic" senses (this appellation is meant, here, onto- and metaphysico-historically; cf. the treatise on *Plato's Doctrine of Truth*,[2] 1941).

Humanism, or anthropologism, is the ultimate human mode of appearance of planetarism; in this, the long-hidden essential sameness of historiography and technicity comes to issue, in the form of the devastation of the globe.

14. The Telling of Difference

Telling is: 1. A naming of inception.
2. A provenance from the inner incipience of inception (tellingly).
3. A poetizing that is more inceptive than every "poetic" and every "metaphysical" word.
4. Itself evental; not an artifact.
5. Inexpressible, each time inceptive.

Therefore the word "telling" is being used here quite simply and does not mean a form of communication. The naming conceals what labeling with names makes

2. *Wegmarken* (GA 9), edited by F.-W. von Herrmann (Frankfurt am Main: Vittorio Klostermann, 1976), 203–38, translated as *Pathmarks*, edited by William McNeill (Cambridge: Cambridge University Press, 1998).

public. In the telling, which belongs to the receding, there is always vouchsafed a possibility of shelter; concealment, always, is protected and especially so, and so too, more inceptively, is the first inception.

Thus "*difference*" [*Unterschied*] is the word of "*separation*" [Ab*schied*] and "*reced*ing" [*Unter*gang].

The telling-ness of this language.

The word of telling is never a statement in the sense that it (the telling) can account for and exhaust what is to be named. But this inexhaustibility also does not mean that there might be some remainder left over which might be diminished over time in the saying. Telling is a statement in the sense that it says inception inceptively, always in an inceptively veiled way. In all interpreting there is a uniqueness, the essential weight of whose truth is that the interpretation is history-grounding, meaning that it makes necessary another interpretation, one that is just as inceptive, but other than it. (By contrast, historiographical construal is assiduous in making every further explanation superfluous.)

The word of telling never itself knows "what" it says, if by the "what" is meant a represented totality of singularities that an inception conceals within itself.

But the word of telling can be tuned by the attuning voice of the unsaid. Thus is the telling and its word what is properly to be heard, a hearing of the unsaid, bound in listening to the inception, receding into it, historical.

Recognize that in the correspondence of the essential relation between beyng and the essence of the human, what is required, necessarily, is an acceptance of the historical non-essence of this relation at the end of metaphysics. Therefore, on the same ground that makes "necessary" the saying of inception, "the human" must also be immediately and continually named. The initially insuperable appearance of the anthropological is to be accepted. And so too must the continual weakening of the telling, even its occasional distortion into the "existentiell." This is only one of the many forms of humanism.

Strange is the telling, in its essence, and thus it remains open as a task.

There is no statement, here, as in a secure and recognizable arena. But it is also not a matter of the arbitrary setting-down of what, without hint or direction, remains simply "incomprehensible." Nor, though, is it a matter of a comprehensibility that would seize hold of what is understood merely in order to dispose of it right away.

What there is, here, is the *crossing* into inception.

15. How Saying Becomes the Acknowledgment of the Event of Inception

Only thus: that being, that is, the beingness of beings, that is, the releasing of beyng into the abandonment of beyng, that is, beyng as event, that is, inception, that is, receding, is inquired into and asked after.

One path of this saying is the telling of difference.

It—the path—must emerge from the *differentiation*. But in order that this be acknowledged, what must be experienced is a sojourn in the human.

The sojourn is that of the essence of the human as historically metaphysical (planetarism and idiocy).

The insidious appearance of clinging to the human is grounded in the essence of metaphysics; today's anthropologism is merely one of its consequences. (Cf. *Plato's Doctrine of Truth*.)[3]

But even if the abandonment of everything that pertains to the human and its presumptions might be decided on, does the human being not still remain—even in the inception? Must it not, first of all, safeguard its essence there? Is it not there that it first needs help? Not help—but hints. And hints from out of beyng. And these hints bring tidings of the receding—they carry in themselves the necessity of decision. In them, humanity itself parts ways, in the courage of acknowledgment.

The courage-worthiness brings to issue the confrontation of historicality with the lack of history.

Historicality has nothing in common with metaphysics (historiography and technicity). The lack of history, however, is the idolizing of the historiographical for the *technique of mass-organization*.

The sojourn of the human being lets itself be shown first of all through planetarism. But planetarism must from the outset be thought onto-historically, without yet being able to call itself the history of beyng. To planetarism, there corresponds idiocy.

---

3. *Wegmarken* (GA 9), 203–38.

16. The Essential Sojourn of the Human in Modernity
Planetarism and Idiocy

The human sojourns in the abandonment of beyng. And the manner of this holding-itself-in-sojourn is the forgetfulness of being.

Sojourn: 1. That wherein the human persists.
       2. That whereby it settles.
       3. That which constitutes time-space.
         (Historiography—Technicity)

The sojourn is determined in two essential respects, necessarily correspondent:

by planetarism   (Notebooks XV, 17, 20)[4]
by idiocy   (Notebooks XV, 22)[5]

Planetarism does not just mean the encompassing spread of a historical situation across the entire planet but rather the essential ground of that which unfolds as the "sameness" of the human (mass-*organization* in the service of world power, which the essence of the mass itself demands in order to secure for itself both necessity and a means of power).

"Idiocy" does not mean a psychiatric determination of obtuseness of intellect and soul but rather that determination of the historical situation in consequence of which everyone, always and everywhere, recognizes his ἴδιον—his own as the same as the own of all the others—and bustles about either willingly or unwittingly. The onto-historical unconditioned essence of the they is idiocy.

---

4. *Überlegungen XII–XV (Schwarze Hefte 1939–41)* (GA 96), edited by Peter Trawny (Frankfurt am Main: Vittorio Klostermann, 2014), translated as *Ponderings XII–XV (Black Notebooks 1939–1941)* by Richard Rocjewicz (Bloomington: Indiana University Press, 2017).
5. Ibid.

17. The Guide-Words of Beyng
(cf. Summer Semester 1941, Manuscript 16)[6]

(To what extent the guide-words seem to be turned against beyng itself, and at the same time say its representability [comprehensibility]).

The telling of these guiding words says:

Being is difference.

- Difference
  Separatedness
  Appropriative event
  Inception
  Receding
- Parting

The de-parting [*Ab-schied*] of the "is."

The overcoming of beyng as the receding of the nothing.

The tellingness of the saying of beyng.

The *guide-words* as escort in the unexperienced sojourn in the site of the *essence* of the human: in being-there—beyng. Granted, thus, to the human in a quite difficult sense that is, though, essentially necessary.

How, from here on, the step into inception as essence of being?

Through the saying of *difference*.

Difference, though, eventually.

No mere projecting and discarding, not at all, as if being would be that which is projected—where and from whence?

Projecting of inception as its *essence*.

To what extent, through "excess" and so on, incipience is named.

To what extent, through "the emptiest" and so on, *beingness* is named.

What is beingness (οὐσία) in relation to inception? The inceptive non-essence of being.

---

6. *Grundbegriffe* (GA 51).

18. The Essence of Beyng

The differentiation
The difference
Projecting—Thrownness

Happenstance
Event
Inception
Incipience
Receding
Parting
—

The essence of beyng can no longer only be beyng—the essential relation of beyng to the human must recognize the human as nothing but history, and that means as the essential unfolding of truth.

Everything to be left behind in the intimacy of parting.

19. The Incipience of Inception

Incipience is the "essence"; here, this says the incepting of inception. Because inception begins, and because incepting is ever more inceptive (which cannot mean the advancing of mere increase but rather only the particular singularizing into the singularity of an inception): because of this, incipience cannot be named in one word. Moreover, we know hardly anything of the incipience of experientially accessible inceptions. And every time, we come up against the danger of drawing out a "commonality" from inceptions and marking this itself down as inception.

The word "inception" remains polysemic and must maintain this polysemy, because in this way it holds the incipience of inception in the inceptive and never allows inception an explanation or a "conclusion."

"The inception" can say: each and every incepting, and the fissured multiplicity of the inceptions whose singularity is thus in a certain way effaced.

"The inception" can say: each singular inception in its uniqueness. "The inception" can say: the inceptive confrontation of inceptions in the sustaining of incipience—the sustaining that is the essence of history. "The inception" can say: the incipience of inception.

The telling "of/from inception" says all this, and says it without stating what inception is. The telling does not reduce inception, as if it were only a matter of delimiting a concept. The telling is "inceptive," not only because it speaks "of/from inception," but because it remains determined by its incipience, saying the uniqueness of inception in such a way that it does not exhaust it.

What the word "inception" names here, however, cannot be twisted out of a clutched-at definition, but neither can the familiar usage of words offer a clue for bringing to knowing what is to be named and referred to.

In a somewhat arbitrary way, the word "inception" is made use of here as the word for the essential unfolding of beyng itself. But there is a "certain" arbitrariness in this word choice, though, because in truth—in the early morning of thinking—being was named ἀρχή.

20. The Staying

The purest (because inceptive, because receding) manner of staying [bleiben] is staying away [Ausbleiben]. In this [staying away] a singular arrival comes forth. Such an arrival keeps its distance and keeps distance itself away in the parting. Staying away is the pure unconcealment of the advental egress (never ever arrived or arriving). Such an arrival has abandoned beings and has been taken up in the pure staying away. This [staying away] radiates a glimmering of the inceptive dignity of inception. The coming of the egress, unconcealed in the staying away, is the inceptive audacity of the claim through which the staying away, as parting, sends away into un-staying everything that constancy appeared to obtain from beings or that befits beings.

The staying away [Ausbleiben] is the staying [Bleiben] from out of [aus] the parting. This staying away is no cessation but is rather the inner essence of the receding inception.

The sending off [Verabschiedung] of beings does not meddle with them and brings about in them nothing by way of destruction. Entirely otherwise, and contrary to the usual expectations, it is the parting that first lifts up beings into the singular occasion in which they might be raised up out of themselves in order to emerge into the open, something that would otherwise remain denied to them. The sending off is what first brings beings (eventually, not as interdependent) into the uncommonness of their own essential simplicity and newness to beyng.

Eventually, the staying away is the appropriative event of the assigning into the arrival of the egress.

The staying away is not a cessation, but neither, equally, is it mere absence. The staying-far-away [*Aus-bleiben*] brings the egress; it is the advent of the distant in the distance. By contrast, the staying withdraws presce and exhausts itself in this taking away.

21. Inception is the Dignity of Beyng

Dignity is not appropriated to beyng by virtue of an acknowledgment. Dignity is that which first permits an acknowledging, granting it the play-space of its endeavors, which must, though, always fall short of dignity.

Dignity is the incipience of inception; thus, it is also not a characteristic of beyng but is rather beyng itself, in its receding, essential unfolding.

Dignity is, inceptively, beyng as receding inception.

Holding itself in the intimacy of inception, remaining distant from it, turning back into inception, and turned toward this return, dignity is the pure unconcealment of its thus inceptively protected concealment.

Dignity is the letting-be of the receding into the separation of concealment.

Whether or not the open realm of the unconcealment of concealment ever becomes manifest is not a matter of dignity. Indeed, even announcing the incipience of inception becomes inessential. What is uniquely worthy of dignity is just that the telling happens. Only the thinking of beyng is worthy of dignity; that it eventuates appropriatively and nothing else.

The event suffices, and it is not necessary, of no genuinely inceptive need, that a humanity should ever, historically, get something of this thinking in its ear, even through distorted hearsay.

To be sure, inception eventuates the stillness of being-there and, in it, a nameless steadfastness. Apart from that, it does not need "publicizing."

Just that it, the appropriative event of inception, might happen; just the inceptuality of beyng's singular *that*: this suffices for beyng.

Whether beyng, as inter-vening, comes into the open realm of beings or whether, by hap, beings occur, remains always happen-stance.

22. The Ultimate Step of Thinking
(cf. The Dignity of Beyng)

How should this be taken, how should it even be intimated, when thinking has only arrived at an approximation of its provisional essence? But the ultimate step does come, finally, not at "the end," though, but at the proper inception of thinking.

And the ultimate step of thinking leads into the knowledge of beyng; and in this knowledge it becomes evident that it cannot be essential that the telling of beyng is made public—precisely *because* thinking, as eventuated, belongs to the event. The event-character of thinking requires of it an entrance into the stillness of pure incipience.

It looks as if what is eventuated in beings and in their public availability is nothing, nothing more than that which constitutes the process, procedures, and activities of beings.

The ultimate step of thinking is the knowledge of the pure belongingness of this thinking, in its uniqueness, to the singular incipience of beyng.

The ultimate step of thinking is the knowledge that, if it happens in this way, thinking can be the singular acknowledgment of the dignity of inception. Beyng appropriates thinking eventually, rendering it necessary in the most extreme plight of pure, remote acknowledgment. Beyng, in its incipience, has need of thinking, and demands the plight of being-there and, for this plight, has need of a singular humanity. But beyng does not need the recognition and taking cognizance of beings; it does not need beings and their availability and efficacy.

The ultimate step of thinking is a knowledge of the incipience of beyng as of the event; a step in which the knowledge does not move forward toward the recognized or apprehended, diffusing itself as something familiar. This knowledge "remains" unknown. And its "remaining" (*bleiben*)—beyond the familiar, but yet accessible—is a kind of *staying away*, an inceptive assigning into the event.

This knowledge knows itself out of itself, but only in the sense that it thinks beyng, that it insists in belonging to beyng and happens from the projecting of beyng. Because of this, the knowing of itself in itself does not make thinking into something of its own over against beyng. This knowing itself in itself has only one essential consequence, which must be held back in reticence: just when and how the inceptiveness of the incipience of inception eventuates.

If this knowledge were ever to become known, it would not be this knowledge, but it might perhaps be a recollecting into inception or perhaps a lost trace of beyng, one that leads beyond beings.

Because of the inner inceptuality of this trace of beyng, its passing-by might well bring beings into an essential radiance, by means of which they might relinquish all mightiness, and in the counterradiance of the dignity of beyng might rise up into a unique simplicity of their thing-hood. Indeed, this might occur in such a way that the *whence* of this gentleness of beyng, as averse to all weakness as it is to violence, could never be explained from beings.

The passing-by of the trace of beyng must lead into the vicinity of an issuance through which, for beings, a humanity and a divinity would become necessary, such that, in turning to this necessity, a world-history might be configured, one in which the world would let the dignity of beyng simply prevail. This, though, without being exempted from the experiencing and withstanding of both the pain and the tearing-apart of beings that accord with the abyssal nature of beyng.

But for a long time yet we will not find this sign of beyng that inception traces out, because we are still all too far from the presentiment of what thinking is, and that thinking must eventuate in the event.

But we can attempt to think forward toward this thinking.

And we must prepare, that we might be the precursors of this thinking. We say the difference of being and beings.

23. Inception and Concealment

It is because the incipience of inception is the receding into concealment, that beyng must remain concealed as it twists itself free in inceptive inception.

The inceptive essence of beyng can long since have transformed itself, without its having made the slightest difference to the domain of actions and needs.

Beyng must persist in the telling whilst guaranteeing to beings the appearance that it is they that respond to beyng. But only beyng can respond to beyng, and as such, appropriative eventuation must remain a responsivity.

Creative responsivity [*Er-widerung*] to beyng is being-there.

24. "Concealment"

from out of the essence of ἀλήθεια.

Later taken up into *repræsentatio*,

transformed in modernity into the "*closed-up*" (Nature);

Contraction as the root force of "existence" as self-manifesting. All framed by subjectivity and "certainty."

*

In contrast, concealment as forgetting of being.

The history of metaphysics as the truth of *beings in their priority over being.*

Modern metaphysics included therein.

Concealment as event *not to be confounded* with the metaphysics of the absolute! *Phenomenology of Spirit.*

25. Inception and Truth ("Eternal Truths")

Inception "is" the essential unfolding of being. Beyng "is"—is itself conceived in incipience.

The essential unfolding of being in the first inception is the unconcealing, the unconcealment. (Truth)

Thus "truth" belongs to the essence of beyng and must be thought only from this.

But meanwhile the commencement of metaphysics brought about the transformation of truth (of its essence).

As distinctive mark of recognition, it enters the precincts of the human, wanting *this* now to become the measure of truth or for human action and its "truth" to measure out what is "true."

The "true" instantly becomes that which gives continuity, stability, and wholeness to the human. In the "true" lies all continuity-giving. Truth is itself what is properly continuous. The most continuous continuance, according to this calculus, is eternity. "Truths" are "truths" as "eternal."

The metaphysical thinking of truth is, thus, in multiple respects, bound by the question of "eternal truths," and the "problem" of "relativism" presents only the flip side of this assertion of "eternal truths."

And to be sure, relativism does obstruct not only any sort of doctrine about the "eternity" of truth, but every question about the proper essence of the essential singularity of truth. This, in terms of the incipience of beyng, is each time one and singular, but not in such a way that it only holds "for" a "time," in which case "time" would become the measure and the arena of play of "validity." Truth itself, indeed, determines "time" for a time, and to each and every time. How, then, should this ("time") take upon itself the role of measure-giving for truth? Truth is determining, but it is not thus that it achieves validity, nor is it, in itself, valid for –.

Truth unfolds as being, which lets beings be, without influencing, thus raising (eventually appropriating) them into the essential unfolding of being. To ask whether this should or must "be" temporary or for always is a meaningless question, one that has already forgotten that it is dealing solely with the essential unfolding of beyng.

So what does the proposition of onto-historical thinking mean, then, that truth "has" a history? This formulation is a poor one, because it assumes that "truth" might initially be an in-itself that would, then, be subject to continual change.

The proposition means far more: the essential unfolding of truth—the manner, in each case unique, in which truth takes place—is the fundamental trait of all history. For history is not the succession of some processes and incidents. History is the sustaining of the essence of truth, a sustaining that itself has the character of event, and this is beyng.

The proposition (that truth "has" a history) does not mean that truth is only "the true" and that the certainty of this in each case is a stage of consciousness. This is how Hegel thinks "truth"; he does not think at all in the domain of the essence of truth but rather, as with all metaphysics, holds it decided that truth is the essence of the true.

26. Beyng and Singularity and Truth

The unity and cohering-together of history is determined from the oneness of beyng. *In* the singularity everything is always singular and only *thus* corresponds to a one. What grounds essential connections to history is not the universality of a multiplicity (metaphysical), but rather the singularity of the simple. "Historiography" can be determined anew only out of *these* connections, provided it hasn't lapsed altogether into metaphysics.

Singularity is the inceptuality of inception. Inception *is* ever singular; this singularity does not exclude the "multiple"; "the multiple" is already just an appearance that, in re-presenting, covers up the singular.

*

Being itself is concealment.

What is this?

Only because being unfolds such that it is unconcealment in beings, can unconcealment (γένεσις-φθορά) primarily and inceptively appear as being—can the appearing itself reveal the essence of being.

Truth
Plato's interpretation is true
Descartes's interpretation is true
Each *only* "of its time"—"historical"—"relative"—
No!
but especially *not* "only,"
rather the opposite: in entirety belonging to one—
the essential unfolding of beyng—the essential unfolding of truth itself.

The truth of the true.

27. The First Inception

That which is entirely strange but nevertheless most proper, of which "we" are not and cannot be in possession, but by which we abide.

In this estrangement we experience concealment as the essence of being.

In the inceptiveness of this first inception the history of being emerges, and the simpleness of all historiographical multiplicity becomes experienceable.

This oneness remains incommensurable with all otherwise familiar relations: the first inception and the history of beyng as "*metaphysics.*"

28. Inception

That being as unconcealedness is emergence, without unfolding into concealment, declares that inception is what has still barely begun.

Inception still remains ahead, and therefore the receding is more singular than before.

Because of it, beings in all their machination cannot be what is constant and cannot unsettle being from its essence.

For that reason the incepting comes first.

But it comes as being.

No investigation of beings makes possible an encounter with being. Every such contrivance remains empty.

29. Event

is, here, naming being, the meaningful and load-bearing word.

1. Appropriative eventuation: Opening-up of the propriative, directing itself into this—to incept.
2. Appropriative eventuation: Creative essence of intimacy.
3. Appropriative eventuation: Sheltering of what is most proper (as proper domain) in what is proper—nihilation as leaving-out the in-between from the proper domain.
4. Appropriative eventuation: The dedicating into properness of the evental—namely: being-there.

5. Appropriative eventuation: Assigning-over into what is proper (beings to being).
6. Appropriative eventuation: History—"appropriative event"—the inceptive "that..."
7. Appropriative eventuation: To essence entirely from out of the most proper—(dismissing every craving and spurning every solicitation).

*

Inception Is Being

Being unfolds
The essential unfolding grants a while
Then, for a while, "beings" "are."

The essential unfolding of being is truth.
Truth is the appropriative event.
The appropriative event passes into ownership
and is the assigning of the there.

The event is inception.
Inception "is" truth.
Truth is being.
Thus, being unveils itself in the crossing.
This comes close to inception.

30. Inception and Intimacy

It is as unconcealment of the open realm of emergence that the inceptive is—an unconcealment, though, that does not disappear but rather, as emergence, remains concealment and protection.

Thus, it belongs to inception not simply to remain within its essence, but to go back into it, always gathering into the more inceptive. This is the intimacy that belongs to the secluded, and is not mere inwardness.

Intimacy is precisely emergence that, before all else, unfolds in presencing, thus returning into itself. Never, though, as "reflection," but as gathering into concealed inceptuality. Inception essences, in that being is ever more inceptive: this says that it is intimacy. Intimacy is the concealment of the broadest unconcealment, the quiescent withholding of the bestowal.

Intimacy is the word for the inceptuality of inception.

31. Beyng

Beyng is inception. Inception is the grounding of the abyssal.

Being, as the first-inceptive inception, is protective concealment (and *therefore* first of all φύσις).

Being, as the first-inceptive ending, is unfettered machination.

Ending is the non-inceptuality of an inception.

Being, as the other inception, is event, the incursive inter-vening that first brings forth the in-between.

The crossing from first inception into the other as inceptuality: the abandoning of the differentiation.

Beyng

as incursion reveals the abyssal unconcernedness of being toward beings.

That is why the human, insistent in being-there can, while yet in the vicinity of utter non-beings (that are never the nothing), achieve the highest sheltering of truth.

To name *inception* means saying "being" and "truth" as *essential unfolding.*

Being "is" truth.

Truth is inception.

Being is inception.

These are sayings of an inceptive sameness: not some sort of line of argument.

32. Inception and the Nothing

The nothing has multiple senses and, like being, is unstable in its history.

1. "The nothing" can suggest nothingness in the usual sense—the complete
    absence of beings.
2. "The nothing" can signify the essence-less as the essential-lack of being.

In (1) the nothing is differentiated by contrast with beings. In (2) the nothing is differentiated by contrast with being (as unconcealment—emergence).

The nothing, here, still does not belong to being itself. In order to know this belonging and find the nothing in being itself, nihilation must be experienced: a nihilation that is not just a negation that places itself opposite being in the manner of a representational placing-before. Being itself nihilates, in that it protects, shelters, and conceals. But this is not a mode of refusal; rather, the "no" is always already said on the ground of the steadfastness of being-there; it is grounded in the "word," and the word is the essential unfolding of being.

Nihilation as concealing is the intimacy of the in-cepting of inception.

Thus, nihilation is also never negativity, which is grounded in subjectity; this latter for its part unfolding in the self-differentiating self-bringing-itself-before-itself.

This not of negativity never releases the nothing into the inceptuality of the abyssal ground.

The not of negativity, and this negativity itself, are already recovered in the unconditioned of absolute knowing and willing.

The nothing of inception, by contrast, is the inceptive nothing, but, therefore, it is also not utterly "void" even though it essentially brings about [*erwest*] the apparent "emptiness" of the in-between of the abyssal ground.

In an inceptive sense, the nothing is the in-between, whose clearing in the differentiation is granted to the arrival as essential site.

To someone who remains outside thinking and who is intent only on explanations (i.e., the pursuit of outcomes and what can be held on to) and for whom only beings have validity as what is essential, one can never even attempt to show that the essence of the nothing is in no way the dissolution into void nothingness, and that if it is taken as such it falls prey to utter distortion.

Whoever does not think, disavows the connection to being. Such a one can therefore never know that it is through the nothingness of the apparent emptiness of the in-between that being veils its essential richness.

But when the nothing persists as the veiling of beyng that belongs to beyng itself (in which veiling the deciding of the difference from beings happens); when, thus, the nothing lifts itself out "beyond" beings and into beyng, then the fundamental attunement, attuned from the nothing, is precisely "anxiety" (taken essentially, not as fearfulness), not, to be sure, an "elated" mood but also not a "depressed" one; rather, attunement raised up into beyng. It rises beyond the thoughtlessness of metaphysics and anthropology and that of all worldviews, into—the nothing, where all is decided.

33. Event and the Nothing

Mere negativity but also the privative and its variant, dialectical negativity, breaks down in the evental essence of beyng (cf. the staying from out of the parting).

Certainly, one can always bring all saying, declaratively, into the framework of mere negation, of affirmative negation, and of deprivation. But if so, there is no guarantee that beyng has been thought or whether, instead, it is still been reckoned only in terms of beings.

But because all the telling appears in the first place to be "statement," and because this appearance can be taken for its most proper being, no thinking of beyng can evade its misuse through "dialectic."

Hegel attempted to save dialectic from atrophying through itself, by urging the broadening of its contents (aesthetics, philosophy of religion, of right, of history). But precisely here arose the flattening-out of the "dialectical"—which is in truth the actuality of spirit itself—into unstoppable formalism.

34. Inception—Beyng—Beings

are, in the first and in the other incepting, Western. And since intimacy—abyssal inceptuality—belongs to the incepting, it is in the West that inception is confirmed.

Confirmed in it and in its singularity, there belongs to inception an ultimate receding. None know of this singularity, just as none are capable of creatively thinking the uncommonness of inception, as if by this we mean a calculation.

In the essence of inception and of its receding there lies concealed, and sheltered as the most extreme intimacy, an ultimate receding. This receding determines an inceptive between-time, in which history does not necessarily continue with the same openness. But this highest possibility of inception—its receding—must, in that receding, also be thought in its finality.

If inception is beyng and beyng essences only inceptively, then beyng itself must (as event) yield "time" (time-play-space), in and with which it itself brings about its receding.

"Then" all possibility of a "then" has vanished; then (still said always and only from *receding relinquishment*), there are also no more "beings." "Non-being," that (said in a relinquishing way) perdures, is neither nothingness, nor is it not nothingness. They "are" that which Parmenides, though *otherwise*, thought in the first inception as μηδέν (but thought in a *more inceptive* sense).

35. Beyng is Telling
(telling word)

What *is* is only in the telling, which means in the word as the domain of keeping silent.

This telling, though, says nothing about beings, but rather says being: it is *telling*, that is, "poetry" in the inceptive sense, which can only be determined out of being itself as event.

Of course, this determination immediately enters into the dubious neighborhood of modern metaphysics. According to this, beings are what is objective, and objectivity is subjectivity.

None of this is valid here, because being thereby remains always just as it does in theological metaphysics, raised-up as a contrivance through the activity of a "subject."

Now, though, what matters is to admit being itself as event; what is more, beyng does not concern itself with this admitting or not-admitting.

36. The Other Inception

The inter-vening as the incursion of concealment itself into "beings."

How the incursion happens as being-there and is event.

How being-there, because it is itself attuned to beyng, unsettles the human from its responsibility for beings and determines him toward steadfastness.

Responsibility for beings and subjectity. All transformation of beings into "spirit" (the intangible and invisible) is still only the forgetting of being.

37. Inception and Ἀλήθεια
(cf. The First Inception)
ἀλήθεια-ἰδέα

How does concealment unfold, such that unconcealing happens and unconcealment (*Entborgenheit*) can unfold as *being*, making it possible, at times, for beings to enter into unconcealment (*Unverborgenheit*)?

"Is" the essential unfolding of concealment the protective concealing in the intimacy of what is more inceptive in the inception?

"Is" this protecting the original safekeeping of the uniqueness of inception's dignity?

And does this "is," and the essential unfolding itself, determine itself for us from out of the inceptive?

Concealment is inceptive, and is therefore never simply occlusion and conservation; rather, it is inceptual, that is, a sheltering into the intimacy of the gathering of that which receives no support in beings and refuses every ground; the gathering of the abyssal ground, the gathering of that which gives to the "there" an abyssally grounding and more inceptive time-space, so that it might eventuate the assigning as being-there.

Sheltering—restraining the thronging and thrusting of beings as they become free.

Recollective forethought, as recollection that thinks in advance, thinks into the first and into the other inceptions, thinks in their fissure; and thinks, hence, transitionally.

In the crossing, thinking is the longing awaiting of being.

But being can never more be established from out of, or indeed as, the human, nor is being to be ascertained from beings, and nor is it to be beheld in gazing at or away beyond beings; being is never to be compelled—crossing is the preparedness for the distant passing-by of the beyond-near.

The crossing does not deny the present. But this present is only historical as the distanced presence that lies far away, because it unfolds in connection with what is to come.

In all this inceptive thinking, though, *recollecting* into the intimacy of inception is what is innermost.

38. The Inceptions

First inception:

Being *is*—(because its essence unconcealment)

The commencement of metaphysics:

The idea is what is most "in being"—ὄντος ὄν

Metaphysics: beings (ens entium) "are" being.

The end of metaphysics: Only beings are and being remains empty smoke, an error.

The receding:

The abandonment of being unfolds as concealed being.

The other inception:

Being is truth, and truth is appropriative event.

39. Inception

as the *inception of thinking* (i.e., of standing-within the knowledge of being).

But "the inception" has in *this* way not been thought in a sufficiently inceptive manner.

"The inception of thinking" does not in any respect mean beginning to accomplish acts of thought.

"The inception of thinking"—involves an onto-historical genitive; the inception, as inception, essentially brings about the clearing, in which steadfastness belongs, as the open.

Inception prepares in itself the sojourn and addresses the human in its essence.

Inception is ever incursive—futurally inter-vening [*dazwischen-künftig*].

The pure, essential unfolding of "being," more inceptive than this itself.

Initially even this name—"inception"—remains ambiguous.

40. *Of Inception*

"The inception" is the essential unfolding of the truth of being. Inception is in every respect more essential than being. In the saying of inception, which first eventuates in the other inception, the step must be risked of leaving behind not only the beingness of beings but also being.

Even the question of being still brings history to the fore.

Onto-historical thinking transforms itself into inceptive thinking.

41. *Of Inception*

In the saying of inception it often (and often only) sounds as if thinking about inception means that the thinking would be the incepting.

This appearance is sometimes unavoidable. It must nevertheless remain clear that it is only being that is inception and is inceptive.

But how the truth of being and consequently the grounding of truth are inceptive, and in consequence of this, how "thinking," too, is inceptive and can be thus named: this can be known only from out of what is inceptive in the other inception.

In the first inception, "thinking" is differentiated from "being," even though what is already revealed there is that they are in every case *the same*.

Inception, strictly speaking, always names being itself, the essential unfolding of which is what we name "truth" and have, surely, long misconstrued.

42. "Inception"

is the word of being that makes it possible to name the first and the other "inception." But "inception" is thought more essentially now; not as the inception "of" and the inception "for" being but rather as the essential unfolding of being itself.

1. Inception and the richness of inceptuality; therefore, the first and the other; yet *we* do not know which is most to come.
2. Inception as emergence and sheltering.
3. Inception as concealing and appropriative eventuation.
4. Inception and history.
5. Inception and singularity.

So the word makes it possible to name again what is named when the guiding words of being are spoken.

But inception *also* the word for being as history—the sustaining of the essential unfolding of "truth."

Inception *also* in relation to progressing, receding, crossing.

43. The Inceptive Essence of Beyng

The intent of saying the "inceptive" is to say that it is only ever as inception that it [beyng] unfolds and that this inception is ever more inceptive. But this does not mean, here, some sort of steady increase but rather the abyssality of the singularity of inception, each and every time.

To name the every time certainly means being caught up in the dangers of historiography.

The inceptive essence of beyng reveals itself from the first inception and in confrontation with it as the other inception, and this is the eventually appropriative inter-vening of beyng as the in-cursion [*Ein-fall*] into beings, which only thus fall into conspicuousness [*auf-fällig wird*] *as* beings. (Cf. *The Overcoming of Metaphysics*[7] and the abandoning of the differentiation.)

---

7. *Metaphysik und Nihilismus* (GA 67), edited by H.-J. Friedrich (Frankfurt am Main: Vittorio Klostermann, 1999), 1–174.

When the eventually appropriative inter-vening of beyng comes to attuning voice and becomes attunement and when the in-cursion into [beings] is thus recognized, only then has thinking immunized itself against continuing to construe this onto-historical thinking "of" beyng in any "transcendental" sense.

Beyng is indeed later and, thus, is precisely not "a priori," though this lateness is never a supplement that follows from beings. For [beings] can never see just how much they themselves have, in beingness, become entirely what is calculated and prearranged.

44. Inception
(*Peculiar Property*) is usually thought . . .

We tend to think [inception] in terms of sequence or consequence; always from out of the no-longer-inceptive. And because this seems to us to be closer, more real and more complete, inception becomes, through and through, that which is *not-yet* . . .

By this means, thinking grasps at most the outset, or else the commencement.

But inception does not itself unfold by letting a consequence follow from it and remaining behind; rather, it unfolds in retreating into itself in the coming-forth of an emergence; in thus falling back, it comes into its own proper domain [*Eigentum*]. The peculiarity of this proper domain [*Eigentümlichkeit*], and the selfhood of inception that is to be thought from it, is what is most difficult and most proper of what it demands from thinking.

From this proper domain—from this retreating into emergence proper (*in which concealment unfolds*)—there arises an essential distinctive mark of inception: that it always immediately releases what has been begun into its essence as constancy and gives to that the semblance of being inception itself. The semblance of inception is what is lodged in the *start*.

Inception *casts off* the incepted from returning in essence: it is this that bears within it the possibility of the releasing into itself of what has been begun.

The releasing of beings into being only "beings" and into no longer needing being.

In this releasing, if it is experienced as this, inceptively and in inceptive essence, there still remains a final resonance of inception.

Why can it come into essence only in another inception?

45. Inception and Advancing-Away

The peculiar property of inception—that it retreats in and into its ownness, in emergence—allows what has been begun [*Angefangene*] to advance away in its confinement [*Gefangenheit*]. What advances-forth turns itself away; inception does not turn from it, for inception, always entirely itself, retreats only into itself.

Inception does not turn away: on the contrary, despite everything, it still turns toward what has been begun, but its turning-toward is the releasing into itself of what has been begun.

What has been begun—is that which, in emergence and its unconcealment, comes to appearance, as if there were no inception, as if there were no essential unfolding of being, which "is" itself only inception.

46. Inception and Truth

In what way inception, in each case, is *in itself* an essential unfolding of truth.

Why, in the first inception, this essence (in accordance with itself) unfolds in concealing itself.

Why this concealing itself remains concealed, hence unrecognizable and therefore unknown.

Why, consequently, the determination of the essence of truth immediately takes another route, so that ἀλήθεια becomes ὁμοίοσις.

Cf. ΑΛΗΘΕΙΑ.[8]

How, in the other inception and its preparation, the essential unfolding of truth comes to decision.

How, from out of the end of metaphysics an essential history of truth opens up: Nietzsche: "correctness": Leibniz: *iustitia*; δίκη—

---

8. *Zum Ereignis-Denken* (GA 73), edited by Peter Trawny (Frankfurt am Main: Vittorio Klostermann, 2013).

47. *Inception and Truth*
(cf. ΑΛΗΘΕΙΑ;[9] cf. Being-there[10])

Truth is not an addition to being, as if it were something that comes into human representing and is adjudged to be above being.

Far rather, the essence of being *is* truth. But truth, here, means unconcealment—as the original opening of coming-to-presence, the bringing-forth of the open that presences in advance.

But unconcealment is sheltering, and sheltering is the concealing safeguarding of the possibility of unconcealing.

Being is truth—in the sense clarified. But this says: being is inception. The inceptuality of inception is the emergent returning-into-itself, the originative grounding of the abyss. Inceptuality is ever more inceptive.

Being unfolding as truth, truth unfolding as the essence of being: this comprises inception. What is said in this manner can never be grasped conceptually with the aid of the familiar and therefore ambiguous metaphysical concepts of "being" and "truth."

Truth is not, here, something that supervenes onto being as a result of a discernment. Truth is the inceptive essence of being. Truth is unconcealment and concealment, and is thus the original unfolding of coming-to-presence, that is, being in the sense of the first inception. Again, "being" is only the first name of "truth." And of course "truth" has been long misunderstood, estranged thus from what is to be said here and always, even now, in danger of being seized hold of metaphysically.

"Being" and "truth" are both inceptive names and name, here, inception itself.

Only now can it be seen what transformation of the essence of ἀλήθεια means:

1. That it comes into the *service* of being as ἰδέα, determining all that follows after it in metaphysics. Plato already accomplishes the first step in the overturning of what is still, to be sure, inceptively ungrounded. Truth is not the essential unfolding of being, nor is being inceptive; rather, beings are able to come into a relation of (representational) conforming to it.

    But this, and all that ensues in metaphysics right up until Nietzsche's equating of being (secured existence) and truth (making secure, stabilizing) is itself only possible because, inceptively, truth is the essential unfolding of

---

9. Ibid.
10. Ibid.

being. Therefore, being and its determination remain at all times within the framework of the reference to truth.

2. Clearly, this role for "truth" appears as the commencement of metaphysics proper. Here, truth is certainty (securing of persistence in the fixity of representing).

Being, now, is also conceived in terms of "truth," but in such a way that it dissolves into "truth" marking out subjectity as what is certain. That being becomes representation does not indicate a mere subjectivization of beings; rather, slipping into non-essence, it is an essential consequence of this: that truth is and always must be the essential unfolding of being. Subjectivization comes from being, which unfolds historically in inceptuality, that is, in truth.

Withdrawal belongs to the inceptuality of inception: the abandonment to itself of what has arisen; the abandonment to the sweeping away of its received essence.

As truth is the essential unfolding of beyng, so must the question of truth, in the crossing from the first to the other inception, be asked inceptively. The thoughtful reflection on the essence of truth in *Being and Time* lies entirely outside the aims of an epistemology or theory of knowledge; neither does it treat of "the problem of truth," in the way this is labeled in "philosophy." Everything is directed solely at the essence of being-there, and this means at the grounding of the truth of being toward the steadfastness of a historical humanity.

Ostensibly, the situating of unconcealment (dis-closure and de-cision) looks like an etymological play on the word ἀ-λήθεια.

Nevertheless, even if the inceptive relation of truth to being is still to remain concealed for some time, the question of truth must still be asked in the crossing and asked in the ambiguous form of the "problem of truth in itself." The question of the question of truth prepares the insistent steadfastness in being-there.[11]

Truth [*Wahrheit*], in its essence, is inceptive protecting [*Wahre*], because this essence is being itself; it is unconcealment, concealment, appropriating eventuation—and this is inception.

---

11. Lecture course, *Grundfragen der Philosophie: Ausgewählte "Probleme" der "Logik,"* winter semester 1937–38 (GA 45), edited by F.-W. von Herrmann (Frankfurt am Main: Vittorio Klostermann, 1984), translated as *Basic Questions of Philosophy: Selected "Problems" of "Logic"* by Richard Rojcewicz and André Schuwer (Bloomington: Indiana University Press, 1994).

48. The Inceptions

always name their fissured singularity; though the saying of both still awakens the desire to figure out connections and even dependencies. But this is precisely not what the inquiry should bring to thoughtful reflection. In each and every singularity, therefore, the same must be named—but inceptively, without relation.

The fissured singularity of inception means that in each case inception is separated from inception by a fissure, and that the fissure does not exist in itself beforehand but rather arises in inceptuality (cf. the *Intimacy of Inception*).

49. Truth and Straying

Truth is unconcealing concealment. As the clearing, it is thus, in itself, at the same time the stray and the misleading: for unconcealment is able to tender itself from and for itself, leaving concealment aside as its other or as something overcome.

Thus, unconcealment is in itself a way that leads away from concealment, and in this very "away from" already shows a straying, that in essence busies itself and lends the open to this busyness. In the same way concealment, taken in itself, can indicate a way that leads away from unconcealment.

Truth, as the unconcealed concealing, is essentially and each time a straying.

And straying is no lack "in" truth and no deformation, but rather an essential distinguishing mark of the inceptive, as which truth unfolds.

The straying, inceptively, is also not the reversal of truth; rather, it is the abyssal grounding of the inceptive. Hence to label straying as non-essence (in the 1930 lecture on truth)[12] is still to cling to the initial guiding approach familiar to ordinary thinking, that knows and takes the differentiation of "true" and "false" as something objectively present "in itself."

Straying is the ground of the possibility of non-essence within essence, such that non-essence does not just remain detrimental to essence.

Hence, if the straying belongs to the essence of truth and truth is the essential unfolding of being and if, from out of this essential unfolding, being is in

---

12. "Vom Wesen der Warheit," in *Wegmarken* (GA 9), 177–202.

each case historical in beginning as a decision about the essence of truth, then, at times, straying must come to the fore in beyng, and the unleashed straying [*Irre*] must determine the truth of beings (their "sense"). *Sometimes, madness [Irrsinn] must unfurl into the world.* And then it must be seen whether a humanity reckons only on beings or whether it is sufficiently inceptive to think from out of beyng.

50. Unconcealment
Ἀλήθεια

as being, is original unfolding of the presencing of the open, in the openness of which presence itself comes to presence.

Unconcealment is more inceptive but also more concealing and, therefore, more concealed than presencing.

Presencing is more inceptive (as emergence and retreat) than presence. Presence is more inceptive than constancy.

Constancy is more inceptive than objectivity.

Objectivity is more inceptive than mere certainty.

But *this* inceptiveness (as being) has long been advancing away from out of the first inception and can still not disavow it.

51. The Inceptions

The first inception:	The being of beings is what is. (The telling)
	ἔστιν γάρ εἶναι (*it presences*, that is, as the presencing of what is present)
Metaphysics:	Beings are, and their beingness consists in . . . (the statement)
	(The "is" is simply made use of)
The crossing:	Is beyng? (Original asking)
	the "is" becomes questionable and points toward dignity.

The other inception: The appropriative event is. (The word)
(The transforming of power into dignity.
The courage that is inceptively other.
*The courageous generosity of the patience for the dignity of
the destitution of eventuation.*)

In the statement "beings are," *being* has been decided. Being "essences" as being-ness. And the statement is the most ordinary—so ordinary, indeed, that it is not even said anymore, or if it is said, it is considered superfluous. "Beings" suffice, and they themselves reveal everything that "is." By contrast, the first telling— "being is"—still belongs to the future, and what it says is often, without consideration, lumped together with what metaphysics says. Therefore, what the telling demands is a recollecting into the essence of being; this we are capable of only when we have already been addressed by beyng in the transitional question: is beyng? Here, everything is already set up by beyng, and the leap of the abandoning of the differentiation has already occurred.

52. The Inceptions

Because inception is only in incepting—an incepting, however, that only ever unfolds in the singular and its inceptuality—inception is itself its own abundance.

Looked at from the outside, the richness of inception means the plurality of inceptions. But here there is no question of "counting," as each is singular and eludes the leveling-off into however many or however many times. Thus, it is also not a matter of the one-off (which belongs to historiography).

The fissure from inception *to* inception is determined in every case from each one. Every inception is, in its singularity, history.

Now, we know the first inception only in intimation of the other.

In the other inception, the first inception is *more inceptive* and precisely never finished.

The first inception essences more inceptively when its emerging discloses itself (φύσις–ἀλήθεια) as the essential concealment in which ἀλήθεια is grounded.

The precipitousness of every inception.

The un-unifiability of the inceptions.

Being is more inceptive than any god.

To what extent does the other inception already begin in the first inception?

In a concealed way, the first inception *is* concealed-*retrieval*. How else might it be unconcealment.

Concealment, however, is covered over, persisting as what is question-worthy in being.

The *dignity* of inception—only in the other inception.

53. The Inceptions (the gods)
The Crossing (the last god)

The crossing is the passage through the fissure of first and other inceptions. We know only of this. And no law is hereby established in itself for "all" of "history."

In the crossing, it is the end of metaphysics that prevails, and with this, the dawning of the final absence of gods. But this absence itself becomes ambiguous. Reckoned historiographically, it is end and termination, but historically, it is a flight of the gods, and it is this that first determines the precedence of beings in their machination.

At the same time, though, the absence of gods is an inception. But in no way is it the inception of the advent of new gods. The craving-for, the reckoning on, and the awaiting of new gods is only a regress into the end of metaphysics. With the absence of gods, there rises up something more inceptive, the possibility of the advent of the decision about the essence of truth from out of beyng and through beyng.

(*The last god*—still only *toward* the appropriative eventuation of the essence of beyng and unconcerned with the human.)

No longer what is most in being—because beyng, in itself inceptive, unfolds simply, without gradation, *as* inception.

54. *The Inceptions*

Recollecting of the first inception toward the inkling of what has not begun in the other inception. The inkling of the other inception toward recollecting into the first inception.

This reciprocity means the oneness of the confrontation of inceptions in the inceptual, always inceptively related crossing.

The first inception: ἔστιν γὰρ εἶναι (Parmenides Diels fr.6)[13]
viz., What unfolds is the presence of presencing
ἔστιν = ἐόν
viz., being emerges.
i.e., being essentially brings about being (is-es)
as emergence (presencing).
[Being unfolds as unconcealment]
ταὐτό
[Being fulfills the essence of the first inception]

The other inception: Beyng "is,"
i.e., being essentially brings about being as *event.*
Appropriative event: assigning of the in-between
Abyssal grounding of what has been
(Concealment as such)
Coming of the distancing

Inceptuality as concealed distancing
of what has been and what is coming, at once—
the incursion into [beings].

---

13. *Der Fragmente der Vorsokratiker*, edited by H. Diels and W. Kranz (Berlin: Weidmann, 1952), 232.

55. The Inceptions

To recollect into the first inception is to think ahead into the un-pre-thinkable of the other inception.

For recollecting thinks into the intimacy of the first inception and thus thinks that inception more inceptively. This greater inceptiveness, however, is that which is not borne out in the first arrival. Only out of the arrival can the present be experienced as beings, that they are. Only out of the arrival is the dislocation projected into the being of particular beings. This being is machination, and being consumed by this must become the fundamental experience. Horror is the first shuddering distress of the crossing.

56. Beyng as the Other Inception

is the incursive inter-vening of the eventuation of being-there, in which the giving over of beings into beyng becomes historical.

Being-there is the in-between between beyng and the human.

Sometimes (*Mindfulness*;[14] *History of Beyng, Typescript* 74[15]) the incursive inter-vening is named by the overused word de-cision, which is not supposed to say something in the least "existentiell," here, but rather says the sustaining that beyng itself is—the sustaining as the essential unfolding of *dignity,* and as that which allows any being the ripening expectancy of the last god. This name names the receding of divine-ness as the crossing into the other. In like manner the receding of "art," which belongs entirely to metaphysics, is brought to issue.

---

14. *Besinnung* (GA 66), edited by F.-W. von Herrmann (Frankfurt am Main: Vittorio Klostermann, 1997), translated as *Mindfulness* by Parvis Emad and Thomas Kalary (London: Athlone Press, 2006).

15. *Die Geschichte des Seyns* (GA 69), edited by Peter Trawny (Frankfurt am Main: Vittorio Klostermann, 1998), translated as *The History of Beyng* by William McNeill and Jeffery Powell (Bloomington: Indiana University Press, 2015).

THE DIFFERENTIATION
AND
THE DIFFERENCE

57. The Differentiation
(cf. From the History of Beyng
II. Project, Section II
and Typescript Summer 1938[16]
Lecture: "*Fundamental Concepts*"
Summer Semester 1941[17])

What is meant here is the differentiation between being and beings. We speak of "the" differentiation, not because it is the sole differentiation, but rather because, amid all difference, it is the first in rank and is so in every essential respect. It cannot be surpassed in its essentiality, not just because it bears on all "essence," but because it itself *is*, in essence, the essential. Here, then, differentiating indicates the fundamental trait of beyng itself that, as appropriative eventuation, comes forth inceptively into incipience, out of the partedness [*Geschiedenheit*] of the remoteness [*Abgeschiedenheit*], and persists only in this origin.

If we speak of "the differentiation," we are immediately constrained in two ways. The first emerges from a thinking that differentiates, as if it were discovering the differentiated (being and beings) to be differentiable, or else a thinking that lets at least one of them (being) arise by way of an "abstraction" achieved through differentiating; this notion, of course, is a fundamental error.

The other way, which may still estrange, emerges from beyng itself, thinking from out of it and thinking the differentiation as beyng itself.

---

16. "Die Metaphysik als Geschichte des Seins," in *Nietzsche* (GA 6.2), edited by B. Schillbach (Frankfurt am Main: Vittorio Klostermann, 1997), 363–416, translated as "Metaphysics as History of Being," in *The End of Philosophy* by Joan Stambaugh (New York: Harper and Row, 1973).

17. *Grundbegriffe* (GA 51).

In truth, though, both of the ways and what they "see" are concealed because, owing to its endless familiarity in metaphysics, the differentiation has never really been considered, even where it is specifically made use of, that is, in ontology; for how should a being be properly grasped as a being, and how should being be determined, if the differentiation between being and beings were not already basically familiar—familiar like a track already well-worn by long habituated travel. But "the differentiation" remains unheeded, even where it must needs only be taken in this sense, as the self-evident ground of the possibility of ontology; perhaps most of all there because, once this has been opened up and represented, nothing can be known of "incepting"; precisely because in this situation it is least of all possible to realize that the differentiation is inception itself.

If, however, being is never a being, and if nevertheless it is only beyng that properly "is" (is-es) then, as the essential unfolding of being, the differentiation has its own necessity in itself, entirely independently of whether human thinking finds explicit occasion to consider whether it needs and makes use of this differentiation.

Yet the thinking-through of the differentiation becomes easily confused; hence the resort to multiple approaches to suggest the closest approximation to the differentiation.

Thus, the rule of formal thinking obliges grabbing hold of "the differentiation" itself and asking, from this point of view: *What* is it that gets differentiated, here, and in what respect? What is the sameness in the differentiation? In what do the differentiated agree, and where do they come into confrontation in separative-difference [*Unter-schied*]? The questions are correct, if "differentiation" is represented formally as a procedure of thinking, and if thinking itself is taken to be the representing of something, and if we let that something rest in the cheap declaration that it be taken, in an entirely empty way, as *x*.

This formal pondering "of differentiation" appears as the most universal kind, where the differentiation between being and beings would be subordinate to something already pre-determined. But this view is in error. And the ground of the error lies in the thinking that forgets itself by "representing something" and no longer considers what is properly to be thought: that this something, however empty it might be, even equated with the nothing, is nevertheless a thinking of being, and that what "being" means is here precisely what is to be said. And this singularity follows: that what is to be thought—the being of something—does not come to thinking as an achievement of thought, nor equally as a representation, but rather solely thanks to this, that thinking, however roughly grasped, already abides in the open of being and must be held in the projection of beyng itself. But then all formal questions of calculation would be barred; it is a matter of recognizing what beyng itself would have to be, if this thinking were to be possible in its essence.

If, in the first place, thoughtful reflection pauses before the presence of the differentiation of being and beings, then right away we can see that this is not some particular kind of "differentiating," a result of the particular "contents" of that which is differentiated. Far more, this differentiation (i.e., that in it which is properly differentiated and in decisive separation) is beyng itself, the inception of all differentiation. "Dialectic" can do nothing here because it is itself a powerless beneficiary of this differentiation, which is not just empty formal differentiating.

So long as the differentiation is taken to be only the result of a thinking (and of metaphysical thinking, for that matter), there is indeed the necessity of overcoming "the differentiation." And this overcoming must be brought to its proper limits.

In experiencing beings, we are familiar with but do not know being. In thinking being, we think beings at the same time. Beings and being are differentiated and are a difference. But how is this difference itself? Here is the place of a decision.

Does thinking now move toward explaining difference as the result of thoughts that differentiate, or does thinking leap back into its own essential darkness in order, there, to recognize being as what is differentiated?

Given in its first form, "the differentiation" can always be overcome. And yet this fails from every point of view to recognize that it is beyng itself that differentiates, as inception, in the manner of partedness [*Abgeschiedenheit*] into the appropriative event of the clearing in which "beings" arise and first become beings.

But here yet another misunderstanding approaches. When beyng is called the differentiated, this might mean that the differentiation takes place on the basis of an identity of thinking and being, in Hegel's sense. Because being is thinking, and because thinking has differentiation (negation) as its fundamental act, therefore being itself is differentiated. This would be the most serious, because at the same time the most subtle misunderstanding of the essential determination, that beyng be inception and event.

Because the appropriative eventuating of the clearing is the essential plenitude of inception, despite the simplicity of this essential unfolding.

The eventuation of the clearing, and the withdrawal of incipience into its abyss, is, of course, separated by an abyss from the representing of something as one thing or another, in which the representing of both is already differentiation, in that one is not the other and the other is not the former. Here, we keep to the representation of empty representing; there, however, we maintain the steadfastness of the knowing of inception and its incipience. Here, in empty representing, is the most common of the operations of human meaning; there, it is the singularity of beyng itself that essences, over which human meaning and human dicta, human acts and human arts, have no power, in that they do not remotely reach as far as the domain of beyng; unless they should give themselves to it in essence, acknowledging the appropriative eventuation of that essence by beyng. But then, the willful game of the apparent ubiquity of formal thinking would be already dissipated and nullified.

But the thinking that is the thinking of beyng must also admit this anew: that "the differentiation," such as it is presented in metaphysics, must be abandoned. There thus arises the appearance of a conflict. The differentiation is to be abandoned and given up. And yet the differentiation is precisely only to be "found" in beyng itself: not just maintained in thinking, but rather in beyng itself as its own most proper domain.

Because onto-historical thinking is in transition toward a going back into inception, and because this crossing is, similarly, also the advancing-away from the first inception toward the essence of inception itself (belonging, thus, to the history that beyng itself is); therefore, it is also necessary, in the thinking-through that serves thoughtful reflection, that this discordance not simply be eliminated in favor of an unambiguous "theory" of beyng; because it is not a matter of the construction of a theory, but rather, simply, of the preparation of a readiness for the acknowledgment of a relation of the human to beyng, a relation that, as history itself, decides the essence of the human.

"The differentiation" thus comes to name that essential unfolding of beyng that is not to be fathomed by enumerating steps, and is not to be presented in theoretical statements but that can even less be given over to a dim "feeling" and "lived experience." "The differentiation" receives the attuning determination of its essence from out of the attunement of thinking, which is attuned through the acknowledgment of the projecting of beyng into the essence of the human, and of the thrownness of this essence into the clearing of beyng—the clearing that (in *Being and Time*) was named "being-there."

The furthest glimpse into the essence of difference in the differentiation is opened up by the following thoughtful reflection:

Beyng is inception and, as inception, it is arrival. But to inception belongs the sustaining of the receding as separation. Beyng is parting. The abyssally inceptive essence of difference is enclosed in the parting. And from here, with some warrant, a step can be risked that otherwise might easily be a misstep:

The essence of difference is not the differentiation; rather, the essence of differentiation is the difference as separation. The discourse of "the differentiation" is, then, only essentially correct if the name names not the activity of thinking but the essential unfolding of beyng, and if this essential unfolding itself eventuates in the event of difference as the inceptive decisiveness of inception into the singularity of its separation.

58. The Differentiation
(cf. Inception and Veil)

Essential thinking is inceptive. Inceptive thinking thinks creatively the differentiation between being and beings, the differentiation that itself belongs to the incipience of inception as the essence of all difference. This differentiation cannot be secured as a resource. It is event. It conceals, over against thinking, the decision of all decisions. It is the concealment of the inceptive and persisting either-or. Inceptive thinking sets up this decision. But not in such a way that this decision and what is decidable is ready and need only be chosen. On the contrary, the simplicity of differentiation and the decisiveness of the differentiable involves a patience in which the truth of inception is first prepared for its grounding into the thinking word, whose essential transformation calls another humanity into saying. The decision is: *either being or beings*—as the fundamental proffering of the essence of truth.

The decision comes from beyng, and unfolds as inception in the event. The decision is not set up by human thinking; rather, human thinking is given over to its essential possibility through beyng: the deciding, the differentiating, the essentially differentiative.

But neither in the first inception, nor in advancing-away from this (in the course of metaphysics) does this differentiation unfold as itself in the essence of its own truth. It is the crossing into the other inception that for the first time yields the happen-stance of the differentiation, initially doing so in the form of metaphysics ("ontological difference" in *Being and Time*). Therefore, the opportunity still remains for evading the differentiation by letting it dissolve into the usual questions of metaphysics, rather than becoming attuned to the event.

59. Differentiation and Inception

Differentiating being from beings means taking up the guiding-thread for the determination of being from beings and their explanation.

Following on from the core difference of metaphysics, beings are either thought in a Platonic-Christo-theological way, that is, causally-demiurgically, or in a modern way, that is, from the representing of subjectity, and are thus "representative" as representedness and certainty. In the completion of metaphysics both explanations of beings are coupled together; being is then will, whether the will of the spirit as idea, the will of love, or the will to power.

Being is differentiated through the differentiation, and thus given up to beings; it remains unclear, thus, who accomplishes such differentiation.

Differentiated in this way, being becomes a result, and must immediately be situated in beings once again. It is either repossessed by an unconditioned being as a product or guide (idea), or else it is stored in beings, as the correlate of a representing.

But being is not the result, displaced and again surpassed, of a differentiation that remains of undetermined provenance; rather, the differentiation is the difference that *seems* to come to appearance from beings: the difference itself belongs to the essence of beyng in its essential unfolding as appropriative event. The difference is the release of the clearing, in which inception—emergent, but catching hold of itself rather than advancing-away—frees itself; the open, before emergence, as it comes to essence as inception, which is the parting that withdraws into itself. In the parting, the separation as difference of appropriative eventuation incepts, and has its singularity in such incipience.

In the event as difference (in parting), beings arise into standing-forth, each according to its own. And through this arising, in accordance with the happenstance of beyng, beings move away from the difference into differentiability from being and, thereby, into possible differentiation.

60. The Differentiation

An attempt might be made, at first, to determine the relation between being and beings directly. Here, two paths present themselves, following the dominant, though undetermined, interpretations of being.

Being is a matter of a distinguishing mark "on" beings: it is what "makes" beings. Thus the differential-relation consists in an interdependency between being and beings. The former effects the latter (as "force"): the latter (beings) are what is real (as the effected), and the former (being) is the real as the effecting reality.

But being can also stand back behind beings, and become just the common "representation" of beings: that which is merely thought, the abstract. In such a case being just remains the way human beings think of "beings," something that "beings" do not even require in order to be. Now being is an effect of a being, specifically of human beings.

Or else, being becomes equated with the objectivity of a being as object, in such a way that "a being" implies nothing other than the objective. Thus, being is a "product" of the actuality of "beings" (affection) and of the being of the "I am" (the spontaneity of "*being*-conscious" [Bewußt*seins*]).

In the end, all these versions of the interpretation of the relations between being and beings are determined with regard to an effecting. This is grounded in the fact that, since the Roman reshaping of ἐνέργεια-οὐσία, the character of effecting and of action has been decisive for beings, whether in the sense of the unfolding of human effective-capacity (imperium), or in the sense of the stipulation of a divine effecting (creatio).

How is inceptive thinking (attuned from out of inception) related to this unexpressed determination of differentiation?

Beyng does not "act upon" beings, nor is it that which is effected through human and divine representing. Beyng is infinitely different from an effecting, and is untouchable by human notions.

Beyng is appropriative eventuation, but the appropriative event effects nothing—it is a giving over and appropriation into the intimacy of its ownness.

As beyng, being "is" itself difference and is never a part or a side of the decisively separate, or one of the differentiated.

61. The Open That is Unnamed in the Differentiation

There is a "between" in the differentiation, but this between remains unnoticed, unconsidered, and unexperienced in the entirety of metaphysics. This "between" is the open, in which a being in each case emerges and stands forth into its ownness, and is thus made available as objectification. (The making available is the essential inception as event into ownness).

The original opening-up of this open is history, concealed, and unfolding as event.

This open towers infinitely, that is, essentially, over every space and every time, even if these are thought as immeasurable in a cosmic sense.

In this towering, though, this open is not somehow "larger" than these regions, but is instead essentially other, without magnitude, and therefore determinable neither from the large nor from the small.

This open is closed to the animal and to the plant, whose "essence," like that of all living things, is surroundings-related, having its own range of operation in which to resonate.

62. The Overcoming of Metaphysics
is
the Abandonment of the Differentiation
(Parting)
(Incursion—Inter-vening)

1. The abandonment of the differentiation does not mean merely giving up on it, ditching it like uninhabitable housing.
2. The abandonment, and *it* alone, opens for the first time the differentiation that, though unthought and uncomprehended, is essential to all metaphysics.
3. This unveiling is accomplished in such a way that what leaps is already the pure saying of being, while still making a leap from the former primacy of beings.
4. Through this abandonment, the differentiation itself becomes de-grounded [*ent-gründet*] (de-grounding means here the withdrawal of the possibility and necessity of grounding, not a destruction of something completed: this grounding was always lacking, a distinguishing mark of metaphysics).

   Metaphysics is losing its essence. The fact that it is publicly widespread, and precisely at such a time, says nothing counter to the end of its history.
5. Despite this, "the differentiation" and whatever resounds in this designation must be thought through essentially.
6. The abandonment of the differentiation implies, to be sure, forsaking the abode, ungrasped, from which metaphysics recognizes the primacy of beings, thus indicating being without taking hold of the differentiation that is decided in such a referencing.

But the forsaking is only the essential consequence of steadfastness in the abode in being.

The leaving-abandoned [*Ver-lassen*] is a leaving-to-itself [*Sichnichtmehreinlassen*] of the primacy of beings and the usual belated consequent of being as beingness in its multifarious metaphysico-historical guises. The belated consequent of being is still there when being is hidden in the *prima causa* (Deus creator).

7. But why is engagement with the differentiation, which remains in any case ungrounded, even necessary? Because only *thus* does the essence of metaphysics reveal itself and is expressly returned to the history of beyng. Only in this history is the overcoming of metaphysics accomplished. Thinking must bear the burden of this returning, though engaging with the differentiation and its abandonment must never become historiographical but rather remain concealed. This does not in the least grant the possibility of a "philosophical position." Accordingly, the thinking of the differentiation thinks decisively from out of beyng, preserving the character of the transitional.

Thus it is, though, that the thinking "of" differentiation soon appears to look to this for the ground of metaphysics, supposing it to be something definite, though henceforth serving only as preparation toward the exclusive saying of being.

8. Thus, the essential insight can arise that, for the differentiation (once secured), it is only as the essential unfolding of beyng itself that what is determined [*Bestimmende*] can be attunedly so [*Be-stimmende*], that is, it can be attuned and, hence, be the attunement.

In such a way the differentiation is recognized and at the same time held back, since it is being itself that takes over the separating, beings appearing only as occasioned in difference.

9. Here, though, thinking reaches at the same time a decisive question that in inceptive thinking takes on a form different from all metaphysics.

The question is raised: whence, beings? But is this not the explanation-seeking, cause-obsessed question of metaphysics? No—because the whence now means only this: how can beings essentially come forth into being? Are beings indeed "before" being, albeit not yet as "beings"? Can this beforeness-of-beings be named at all? (Cf. Event and Beings)

10. Essential insight of the history of beyng: beyng comes later than ["beings"]. Being only ever breaks into [beings] such that this incursion is an *intervening* of an essential kind. It eventuates the in-between itself.

This incursion of being into beings changes nothing at all in these, but just lets beings first *be* the being that, before the inter-vening, was precisely what was concealed in being: its concealing.

This evental inter-vening is of an entirely other essence than the "later than" and the following-after of beingness to beings. The inter-vening can also not be explained by a change in the human, but rather the opposite: the essence of the human gains the possibility of change in being given over to Dasein.

Thought inceptively and onto-historically, ["beings"] can hence [be] *without* being; *then* there is neither concealment nor unconcealment; least of all is there *then* the nothing. The inception of which remains in being. "Then" there "is" also no "then" and no "heretofore." Because "time," indeed, as the *ecstatic* clearing of presencing-being, being-to-come and having-*been* [*An- und Zu- und* Ge-*wesens*], eventuates as appropriative eventuation, not only as the merely successive. *This* is inceptive historicity.

11. In the evental inter-vening, being demands from thinking release from all directions of questioning that cling to the "a priori" and quickly distort be-ing into beingness. [The question of the making-possible!]

But the question of the relatedness of being to beings is not thereby cut off.

The relatedness is itself history and, in a more inceptive sense, *turns*. From being as incursion into (beings), from beings to event, from event to being-there, from being-there to the temporalizing of beings as such.

12. In the historicity of the inter-vening of the in-between, the essence of the *debarring* (ἄπειρον) and *concealment* (ἀλήθεια) first reveals itself.

Here the de-clining [*Rück-gänglichkeit*] of inception, the incepting of the abyss, is first knowable in the knowing that does not re-present but, rather, stands within appropriating eventuation.

13. Accordingly, the saying of beyng in the other inception comes (despite the abandonment of the differentiation) from out of the overcoming, and thus far, there still remains in this saying a suggestion of beings in their meta-physical kind of precedence. The difference does not become effaced. But it is changed essentially.

14. The event-like inter-vening, which is how beyng unfolds in its incursion into [beings], can nevertheless never be said historically-inceptively in its first naming and, thus, in the incepting itself. The first is also a way station here. But what must be risked is the attempt to unfold this way station out of being itself and *as* being. Not in such a way that being would only be the "medium" and the "ether" of the way station. (Appropriative event, inter-vening, and way station.)

15. Without explicit reference to the inceptive inter-vening, the guiding-words of being (Spring Semester 1941)[18] endeavor in general to show this way station only as reminiscence.

---

18. Ibid.

16. At the same time, the inceptuality of being is that which—in *Being and Time* and in the Kant book[19]—were sought as the "finitude" of being. But all this rapidly fell into metaphysical misunderstanding. Moreover, in an entirely metaphysical way, the finite becomes mistaken for the "infinite"; as if the saying of the finite might be explained as a going beyond it; as if the unconditioned infinite of absolute knowing allowed for a finitude only, as it were, in a conditioned manner, as the basis of a sublation; in the end, all that appears is "finitude" in the sense of a crude createdness.

17. The abandoning of the differentiation is the saying of beyng itself from out of the appropriating eventuation into being-there.

The abandoning [*Verlassen*], like the naming and thinking-through of the differentiation, is a still-admitting [*Noch-zulassen*] *of beings* in their difference from being, the difference that here enters into the ambiguity of beingness (metaphysical) and beyng (other inception).

The abandoning, the naming and the thinking-through belong in their unity to the overcoming of metaphysics, the overcoming that is inceptive inasmuch as it remains connected, not simply to the end of *metaphysics*, but to the first inception and to the other inception, placing them in confrontation.

Therefore, the beings that are still admitted are not beings in a general and undetermined way but rather beings as the actual, inasmuch as actuality holds priority over possibility and necessity, and is determined as an always-effected actuality. The veiled distinguishing mark of beings as the actual is the brutality with which what "is" and what is "not" is decided. The oft-named "closeness to life" that is demanded of all beings has the role only of deceptive foreground, in which what "life" means seems to be left undecided. But "life," here, means will to power, that is, machination. The still-ad-mitting [*Noch-zu-lassen*] of beings, unfolding thus in the overcoming, is no falling back on the priority of beings and their beingness but is rather the innermost essence of overcoming. For mere renunciation and rejection are still a binding and a mere isolating. By contrast, the admittance is the mark of other-inceptive steadfastness in beyng. Moreover, this admitting precisely releases beings for the inter-vening as which beyng eventuates.

18. The differentiation of beyng from beings is inception and the ground of the differentiation of essentia and existentia (cf. From the History of Beyng).[20]

---

19. *Kant und das Problem der Metaphysik* (GA 3), edited by F.-W. von Herrmann (Frankfurt am Main: Vittorio Klostermann, 1991), translated as *Kant and the Problem of Metaphysics* by Richard Taft (Bloomington: Indiana University Press, 1997).

20. *Nietzsche* (GA 6.2), 363–416.

The differentiation of beyng over against beings must also, though, already flash up in the first inception, without coming to be known *as* differentiation, *as* the incipience of inception. What else would the differentiation of ἀλήθεια and δόξα be?

63. *The Differentiation and the "As"*

The "as" is the pull in which all difference and "determining" are dragged along. The "as" seems to be "established" and deployed by thinking. But in truth it is the naming of the differentiation, inasmuch as it is the openness, as the essential unfolding of beyng, for all relating and saying.

The "as" is multifaceted. Within metaphysics it names the experience of a being as a being: the determination of a "subject" in a proposition "as" this and that through the predicate; the withdrawal of objects (the standing-against) over against the "subject."

From here on out, the "as" is implied everywhere, in discourse and in wordless relation.

In the face of the misunderstanding of the "as" (qua, ἤ), the only thing that protects is the thoughtful reflection that formal thinking is not inception and ground and measure, but rather end and result and constraint; and that only through its emptiness and essential self-forgetfulness can it claim for itself universality.[21]

---

21. (The as of the twisting-free).

THE INCEPTION
AS
RECEDING

64. Receding

The setting into vibration of inception into the return to the dignity of the self-defending of the abyssal grounding, and toward the intimacy of the sheltering of its proper domain, from out of the eventuation in what is most proper for the concealment of the singular.

The receding is the first (i.e., unique) singularity of emergence into its essence; it is the incepting inception.

The receding *is* the singularity of the event. Event, however, "is" itself no longer a different sort of essential unfolding of being.

If the receding is event, it also cannot be said that being "ceases"; because it does not have duration. Just as little can it be meant that being continues "in concealment," for there is no concealedness beyond the concealing itself.—

Concealment into the most proper is the fulfillment of being in inceptive nihilation.

Concealment is the highest sheltering, entering and receding [*Ein- und Untergehen*] into the proper domain of singularity.

65. Receding and Bestowal

The highest bestowal assigns the safeguarding of the proper domain to being-there.

This bestowal is pure concealment into the intimacy of receding [*Untergang*].

Here, "down" [*unter*] does not mean downward but rather upward into the sheltering ("under" the tensed arch of its dignity).

Bestowal corresponds to no taking hold or craving, only the generosity of destitution in beings attunes being-there.

66. *Inception and Receding* (Cf. Section 90)

Receding is what is ultimate and highest in inception as it enters into its most extreme inceptuality. When this receding is, no one knows. That it indeed unfolds lies in the essence of inception itself. Inception must be a receding. Why? A distinction remains to be made between:

the *transitional* receding between particular inceptions, and

the *inceptive*, that is, ultimate receding as the only, that is, singular incipience.

If receding belongs to the essence of being, then, in receding, inception recedes into its concealment. However, we cannot say that being then becomes nothing, even if we mean by that a void nothingness.

The receding is the enstasis of time; that which is final, the parting "of" inception. But parting is never nothing. It is that inceptiveness of inception, in which the most extreme uniqueness of being first becomes thinkable.

67. *Why and How Does Receding Belong to Inception?*

Does receding consist only in this: that the emergence and advancing-away from inception of a continuation ceases at some point?

Just as start and finish, in themselves and in their belonging together, are particular essential occurrences, so, too, receding is to be expressly determined only from out of inception. Receding does not correspond to the other of inception but is rather inception itself, inasmuch as it shrinks back and does not just emerge in incepting.

68. *Receding and Beings*

The receding relinquishes beings to beinglessness. This receding "relinquishing" is the ultimate that can still be said from out of inception. The beingless is the name for the unsayable. In it, what unfolds is the appearance that beings are henceforth supposed to insist on their own permanence, and this appearance issues insidiously in a view that is really only a regression to the metaphysically groundless re-presentation of something present, to which a special distinction is given (a distinction one believes that one *has* to give) because it can be discovered at every turn.

But being unfolds in inceptuality and singularity, not in the constant continuity of the mere et cetera of an otherwise empty objective presence.

The receding recollection is the separating-away into beinglessness, and through this parting, being is once again safely returned, at last, into safekeeping.

69. *The First Inception and the Receding*

The first inception unfolds solely in unconcealment itself, in such a way that it does not acknowledge concealedness as concealment and pursue the essence of being, but neither does it allow the slightest emergence of the receding essence of inception.

Unconcealedness is the τὸ μὴ δῦνόν ποτε, the never-receding of the emergedness of unconcealment, which unfolds in the emergence.

Here indeed is the inceptive clue for the advancing-away into the ἀεί of constancy.

Otherwise, though essentially the same: the ἕν of Parmenides.

70. Receding and the Other Inception
Crossing and Receding

The overcoming of metaphysics is the onto-historical devastation of beings by the abandonment of being.

This devastation is the *commencement* of receding.

Receding, here, initially means that beings plummet down from their dominance over being—(the inceptive essence of receding).

The receding, long prepared and widespread, becomes suddenly and uniquely the essential unfolding of beyng.

Receding—precisely, though, still lets beings continue (cf. devastation and its appearance); and beyng sinks into "beings" as the inter-vening.

To experience the *receding only* as the uniquely inceptive.

All the latecomers, even the most recent, know nothing of the receding. They operate only in misunderstandings.

71. Receding
(understood as more transitional receding)
cf. Inception as Receding

Only the inceptive can recede, because the receding is the plunge back into inception, yet in such a way that this inception lets another inception begin. Receding is connected to this.

If, though, onto-historically, metaphysics is not inceptive, then it also cannot recede but, rather, only comes to an end.

So long as this end of metaphysics at the same time includes, as its completion, the entirety of metaphysics, and so long as metaphysics is (therefore) the sole possibility of the advancing-away from inception, the receding of the first inception must at the same time conceal itself in the completion of metaphysics.

The concealment announces itself in a crossing to the other inception. This is why all that is first-inceptive, and the entirety of its advancing-away, is now to be determined only from out of the other inception.

II. Inception and Inceptive Thinking the Creative Thinking of Inception[1]

---

1. A section entitled *Thinking and Knowing—Thinking and Poetizing* (cf. Hölderlin Lecture 1941–42) precedes this. [Editor's note: This section placed by Martin Heidegger in *Das Ereignis* (GA 71), edited by F.-W. von Hermann (Frankfurt am Main: Vittorio Klostermann, 2009), 305–20, translated as *The Event* by Richard Rocjewicz (Bloomington: Indiana University Press, 2013), 265–77].

72. The Few Must Restore Inception into the Inceptive

The few must restore inception to the inceptive, even if it is only by way of a narrow path that this might succeed, after long wandering and in still rarer light.

Inception is the need . . .

Each inception is more inceptive than the first, and thus *is* this inception itself in its singular future.

Recollecting into the first inception is never a matter of going back "behind" it but, rather, of going forward, out of its intimacy and into the other inception (receding).

The most intimate inceptuality is the receding.

Inception is the need for the receding.

What is needed beforehand is that the slightest belonging to inception be entrusted to care. From afar, and but darkly, comes the sacrifice that once again, and perhaps for the last time, points the Germans toward belongingness; giving them to know that no purpose holds any longer, that all "goals" engage only a straying into machination, and that all "values" serve only the instituting of devastation.

No longer can it be asked: "To what end?" The simple plight alone is to be knowingly accepted.

Destitution in the inceptive, still concealing inception, ennobles inception without insisting on results. For, as inception, beyng is the essential site of the dignity to which a being is freely given over when the inter-vening of beyng eventuates.

In the moment of sacrifice, the question of "To what end?" might often impose itself. But the sacrifice has no need, now, of a purpose. For it is in itself the appropriative eventuation of the essence of beyng, however long unknown and long misunderstood. Calculation and contentment in what has gone before support, in their way, the misunderstanding of sacrifice. But at the same time, they exclude sacrifice, in that they do not let its simpleness—the event-character of the beckoning into belonging—be experienced but, rather, instantly resort to explanation.

73. Inception

When we no longer have need of a sign and no longer seek to scramble for an effective foothold in something signaled, then we enter into the beginning of preparedness for inception.

But, as always, most are still in need of "images." Only rarely do individuals draw out beyng from the imageless word.

And sometimes this word loses itself in images, lingering there in the same presence, like a star that, turned to us, still turns itself away for an infinite span into the darkness of the inceptive.

74. Onto-Historical Thinking

thinks inceptively and thinks only the inceptions; it thinks incipience, and has thus inceptively acknowledged beyng's return to safeguarding. The inceptive recognition of beyng consists in the "overcoming" of its essence, a twisting-free into inception.

Onto-historical thinking does not want a forgetting of being, but rather its twisting-free into incipience.

Inception incepts being.

Inception, as receding, twists beyng free.

Inception "is" beyng, which is to say that its incipience twists free the "is" and beyng.

Onto-historically: this means the entrance of beyng into history as the event of inception.

75. The Onto-Historical
Thinking of Inception

lets inception unfold as beyng, and incipience unfold as the essence of beyng, and this means: to incept.

This incepting, which is not produced by thinking but is far rather that from which thinking is eventuated, unfolds as receding.

The overcoming of metaphysics is only the start of the overcoming of beyng, which recedes into its inception, becoming a receding toward the intimacy of the parting.

But the overcoming of metaphysics is the necessary foreground for the rising-up of the history of beyng, into which beyng itself recedes.

The event of inception is the singularity of truth in the receding toward the parting.

The overcoming of metaphysics is the prelude to the twisting-free of beyng.

76. The Claim of Onto-Historical
Thinking

We stand in preparation for onto-historical thinking. And this preparation can only minimally will, because its "will" is an essential kind of a patience, one that derives from the nature of being-there as already eventuated appropriatively. What can be minimally determined is that the following might yet be attained for the history of Western man: the transformation of the essence of the human, from out of the relation to being, through and for being, into relation with it. The freeing from the supremacy of beings and their abandonment of being remains the closest singularity. The least is already enough: because in it an acknowledgment of the dignity of being must already eventuate.

This acknowledgment of being is not only historical as the thinking of the first inception, which comes out of this and continues in its unconcealment. Acknowledgment is the recollecting into the intimacy of inception.

Slight is the claim, but nevertheless, in corresponding to the essence of inception, thinking must already think ahead into the highest extremity of the intimacy of inception and know the receding that belongs to inception. It could hardly be borne by ordinary ears, were one to call onto-historical thinking what, as inceptive thinking, it must be. Onto-historical thinking is receding thinking. This cannot be compared to any historiographical ambiance of decline, which clings only to perishing and ceasing, to impotence and collapse, reckoning this up merely as ending.

But equally extraneous, and purely historiographical, would be the point of view that looks to rise up, by contrast with perishing, thus consoling itself for the direness of the ceasing of what has gone before.

In all this, onto-historical thinking must be sufficiently insistent to think in advance of the receding as the most proper of events, and never let it from thought.

Onto-historical thinking thinks into the inceptions, and thinks from out of the confrontation of first and other inceptions.

The first inception is the emergent and advancement-preparing inception (ἀρχή as the configuration). Advancing-away points into the crossing.

The other inception is the receding inception that prepares the parting. This is the inner incipience.

The other inception is the inceptively incepting inception.

The Crossing into the Other Inception

The first preparation for the crossing, which itself remains eventual, comes up against barely surmountable obstacles, because it is a matter of thinking ahead into being itself, and that means appropriation by beyng itself.

One help is the recollection into the first inception, because this makes it possible to show unconcealment as the essential unfolding of being. But this— the recollection—lingers under the suspicion, barely to be overcome, of being merely historiographical and hence still "subjectivistic," some contrived bringing-to-mind. But the thinking-ahead into being, which sallies forth from the sojourn of the age, everywhere runs into the appearance that being is really always what effects—thought in a modern way, it is the will—and thus beings would "be" what are effected, produced, objective, and intended.

It is the Christian interpretation of beings that bears the broadest, and still barely gauged, responsibility for this ossifying of the truth of beings, according to which they remain something produced. Thus, it is especially curious that "Christianity," and what calls itself this as metaphysics, needing one day to rebel against "power" (although being as power *is* the true-born and direct lineal descendant and inheritor of the Christian production-oriented interpretation of beings), deems its explanation to be the supposedly sole way of knowing beings (corresponding to the domination of cause in the determination of being), the explanations of science (of modernity in its entirety) being only the other side of that interpretation.

Christianity and modern enlightenment of whatever kind have brought the greatest ruin into the truth of beings, demanding beings' forgetfulness of being. As both of these begin to establish themselves in increasingly unmistakable combination as the planetary world-interpretation, thinking ahead into being itself is brought here before its highest obstacle. Despite this—

77. From Inception

To speak from inception means bringing the inceptions to a sustaining, letting each emerging and receding inception incept into its "essence."

The sustaining as an allowing-to-ripen and, at the same time, a carrying [*Hintragen*] toward each particular inceptuality.

The sustaining is especially the recollection into the first inception and the thinking-ahead into the other inception. Task: to present recollection as such through a simple interpretation of the first inception.

To convey the thinking-ahead in itself through a passage into the receding and properly incepting inception.

The recollection leads beyond οὐσια-φύσις back into the unsaid of Ἀλήθεια as ἀρχή.

The thinking ahead advances into the event of receding into the parting.

In this thinking ahead there is, essentially:

The twisting-free of beyng, in such a way that it will be said in the saying of the difference.

The thinking ahead stands under the sign of the inceptive question-worthiness of beyng [beyng?].

Between inceptions there is metaphysics as the history of the truth of beings. Toward this advances the emergent inception. The going-(away)-from [*Fort-(Weg-)gang*] out of the first inception begins with the subjugation of ἀλήθεια by the ἰδέα (cf. *Plato's Doctrine of Truth*).[2]

---

2. *Wegmarken* (GA 9), 203–38.

Metaphysics points into the crossing to the other inception, though only for thinking-ahead as inceptive thinking. In the crossing, the differentiation of beings and being must be fathomed, and the essence of truth specifically inquired after (cf. *On the Essence of Truth*[3]).

The sustaining of the inceptions is obstructed by metaphysics.

The sustaining cannot be brought about retrospectively through a thinking, for instance in the manner of a "dialectical" opposing and working-over.

The sustaining eventuates the rigorous fissure of the inceptions in their singularity.

The recollective thinking-ahead stands in the site of the crossing and speaks from a knowing whose essence is silent speculation [*Vermutung*]: the intimating creative questioning of the inceptions, which attunes all dispositional courage [*Mut des Gemüts*].

The intimating inquiring has "thoughtful reflection" as its preliminary stage. But this cannot contribute in the slightest to the event of inception. And so, even the saying of fore-thinking recollection, just as the saying of recollective fore-thinking, remains only ever a gentle guide, coming from afar, toward the evental appropriation of historical mankind into the site of being-there.

The recollecting into the first inception never makes this "comprehensible." It estranges, awakening the experience of the cutting off, though his history, of metaphysical man from this first inception, but also the experience of being at a standstill before the withdrawnness of the other inception, for as long as he sticks obstinately to metaphysics and its variants.

Thinking ahead into the other inception cannot bring this about but does indeed beckon into the place reserved for the essence of historical mankind, which withstands the crossing into the receding inception.

Thinking ahead is an inkling and is always also recollective.

The inkling—recollectively thinking ahead

The inkling—sustaining the abandonment of being*

The inkling—striking at the plight of the absence of plight

The inkling—releasing all metaphysics

The inkling—imposition of disposition

The inkling—naming of being-there

  (cf. The Saying, typescript p. 11)[4]

   The sojourn of the current epoch.

*If one were to identify the abandonment of being historiographically, one would have to make use of a historiographical label and speak of planetarism: here, this

---

3. Ibid., 177–202.

4. Cf. *Zum Wesen der Sprache und Zur Frage nach der Kunst* (GA 74), edited by T. Regehly (Frankfurt am Main: Vittorio Klostermann, 2013).

would mean that everywhere across the earth the historical essence of the present is the same, impelled thither in order to nihilate the indestructible in devastation.

One label, of a historiographical sort, for the devastation would be "Americanism." The historical essence of planetarism also contains a decision of a unique kind, whose either-or runs thus:

Either nihilation or devastation. Nihilation in each case and in every respect.

Recollecting and thinking-ahead cannot be separated from one another; one demands the other, and the courage for this thinking finds no clue, unless it be in the appropriative eventuation into being-there, into whose site humanity and divinity is gathered in receding.

Every thinking-ahead is a giving to recollection. And every recollection is the grace of a thinking-ahead.

As a thinking that is inceptive and receding, recollective thinking-ahead is beyond metaphysics. This is a matter neither of a "historiographical" nor of a "systematic" conception; nor, as in Hegel and played-out metaphysics, is it in any way a systematics of history.

But metaphysics, in the mortal ossification of its non-essence, for a long time to come will maintain a hold over meaning, and that means maintaining a hold over the indifference toward what has been unquestionable in the essence of truth. Therefore, thinking in the crossing must also keep this in knowing: its transitionality [*Übergänglichkeit*].

78. Outline
(Outline rather than pure saying)

The first inception:	Ἀλήθεια—φύσις
	Anaximander, Heraclitus, Parmenides.
Of advancing-away:	Concealment of being as releasing of beings; (the differentiation).
Metaphysics:	From the history of being.
	ἰδέα—will to power.
Of the crossing:	Being's abandonment of being; the plight of the absence of plight.

The other inception: The event as the sole incepting inception.
Of the receding: Being-there as the site of inception and parting.

[*Contributions,*[5] *Mindfulness,*[6] *Overcoming,*[7] *History of Being*[8]—take up here]

79. Outline of the Telling of Inception (Outline Rather Than Introduction)

Beyng? A passage into the incepting inception (thinking ahead).
Ἀλήθεια A passage into the inception as it advances away (recollection).
ἰδέα—*Will to Power*—A passage through the history of the truth of beings.
(Recollection that thinks ahead as the sustaining of inceptions.)
The site of inception—Being-there.

Beyng?
A passage into the inception as it incepts
(Thinking-ahead in the sustaining)

The sojourn of the essence of modern humanity in played-out metaphysics.
The establishment of played-out metaphysics as "world-view."
The designation "world-view":
The establishment of the essencelessness of truth.
Thoughtful reflection as really meaningless.
Planetarism.
Idiocy. (cf. Notebooks XV)[9]

---

5. *Beiträge zur Philosophie (vom Ereignis)* (GA 65), edited by F.-W. von Herrmann (Frankfurt am Main: Vittorio Klostermann, 2009), translated as *Contributions to Philosophy (of the Event)* by Richard Rocjewicz and Daniela Vallega-Neu (Bloomington: Indiana University Press, 2012).
6. *Besinnung* (GA 66), edited by F.-W. von Herrmann (Frankfurt am Main: Vittorio Klostermann, 1997), translated as *Mindfulness* by Parvis Emad and Thomas Kalgary (London: Continuum Books, 2006.
7. "Die Überwindung der Metaphysik," in *Metaphysik und Nihilismus* (GA 67), 5–103.
8. *Die Geschichte des Seyns* (GA 69), edited by Peter Trawny (Frankfurt am Main: Vittorio Klostermann, 1998), translated by William McNeill and Jeffrey Powell (Bloomington: Indiana University Press, 2015).
9. *Überlegungen XII-XV* (GA 96).

The ungrounded ground of metaphysics is concealed in the un-interrogated differentiation of beings and being.

The unfolding of the differentiation from the essential modern sojourn of the human (cf. Guiding-words, Summer Semester 1941).[10]

The differentiation unfolds in the difference.

The difference is the essential unfolding of beyng.

Beyng is the in- and ac- cidence [*Ein- und Zu-fall*] of the inter-vening of unconcealment as clearing.

The inter-vening and "beings" before the arrival.

Beinglessness of [beings]; beings as the nothing-less.

Incursion as appropriative event.

The appropriative event is the incepting inception.

The incipience of inception consists in this, that the first inception, advancing-away into metaphysics (configuration ἀρχή) across the abyss that only now becomes properly abyssal, catches hold of itself and, in this intercepting, steps back into the receding.

The receding takes what is first-inceptive in the simple emerging (ἀλήθεια—φύσις) back down into the dignity of the intimacy of concealment that, as such, is only now inceptive.

The receding is the twisting-free of beyng.

The twisting-free of beyng is the parting into inception, is inception as parting.

The parting is the intimate incipience of the difference.

The twisting-free of beyng is the inceptive overcoming of metaphysics.

The convulsion of the *essence* of historical man has begun.

Ἀλήθεια
A passage into the first inception (advancing from)
(Recollection in the sustaining)

The saying of Anaximander: ἀρχή—ἄπειρον—ἀλήθεια
The saying of Heraclitus: τὸ ᾐ ἢ δῦνον ποτε.—
(φύσις—λόγος—ἕν—πῦρ)
The saying of Parmenides: τὸ γὰρ αὐτὸ . . .

The first inception as unconcealment into the emergence toward presencing. Incipience as configuration.

Incipience and history (history of being).

Recollective interpretation as thinking ahead.

The advancing-away of the first inception toward οὐσια—ἰδέα.

---

10. *Grundbegriffe* (GA 51).

ἰδέα—ἐνέργεια—*actus*—*actuality*—*will to power*
A passage through
the history of the truth of beings
Metaphysics
(cf. Toward the History of the
Concept of Existence)[11]
(Nietzsche's Metaphysics)[12]

The beginning of metaphysics and philosophy:
Plato (allegory of the cave)
Aristotle (Phys. B1 and Met. Θ10).
The reshaping of metaphysics in the Roman.
The theology of Christianity.
Descartes (*verum als certum ens*; *subiectum* and system).
Leibniz (*monas—repraesentatio—universum*).
Kant (Being as objectivity—the transcendental).
German Idealism
Nietzsche's Metaphysics.
The completion of metaphysics and its transformation into "world-view."
The crossing into the other inception.
The sustaining of the inceptions.

The Site of Inception
Being-there

Incipience and the receding history of humanity.
Incipience and the receding history of divinity.
The parting and the disposition of being-there.
Steadfastness in the disposition and guardianship of receding.
The parting and unique singularity of beyng.

---

11. "Zur Geschichte des Existenzbegriffs," Freiburg Lecture, 1941; *Vorträge* (GA 80.2).
12. *Nietzsche* (GA 6.2), 231–300. *Nietzsche III: The Will to Power as Knowledge and Metaphysics*, edited and translated by D. F. Krell (New York: Harper and Row, 1987), 185–254.

80. Of Inception
(Setting Up of the Telling)

The first inception—(being as *emergence*)
> Anaximander, Heraclitus, Parmenides.

The advancing-away from the first inception
into the beginning of metaphysics (Plato).
Metaphysics as the history
of the truth of beings (What-being—That-being   Toward the
> existential   History of the
> Concept of Existence).[13]

The ending of metaphysics in the receding
of the first inception—(Nietzsche, being's abandonment and the concealment).
Receding as crossing
into the other inception—(the differentiation of being and beings and the giving
> up of the differentiation).

The other inception—(Being: the incursive inter-*ven*-ing of appropriative even-
> tuation).

Of inception and the inceptuality of thinking.
The inceptive receding.

81. Of Inception

that is, from the emergence of the essential unfolding of the truth of beyng into
the history of beyng, toward the other inception.

This is more inceptive than the first, even though within its mandate, both in
its subsequent effects and in essence.

Inception is, in that it becomes ever more inceptive. This increase not grad-
ual, but the intermittence of the always inceptive, of the singular.

---

13. "Zur Geschichte des Existenzbegriffs" (GA 80.2).

Inception into inception has in itself the between-history of the priority of beings over being, as beingness. This between-history is the history of the truth of beings as metaphysics. *Inception into inception is the receding.*

From inception, a pure saying shall be attempted such that, always and everywhere, beyng itself, in its truth, attunes history and announces the preparation for being-there.

Being-there is the in-between, through which inception is taken up into its essence, so that, in being-there, steadfastness in the truth of beyng finds its grounding for the transformation of the human domain.

From inception into inception is to say, without any adornment, but within the transformation that was attempted in *Contributions*,[14] in *Mindfulness*,[15] in *The History of Beyng*,[16] and in *The Overcoming of Metaphysics*,[17] in addition what is essential concerning ΑΛΗΘΕΙΑ.[18]

But the saying must encounter a fundamental attunement toward inception, in which the voicing of the concealing reticence comes to attunement, so that, in advance, there be a dis-placing into being-there.

82. *From Inception*
(Belonging to the Clearing of Beyng)

Where "philosophy," as in the metaphysics of German Idealism, becomes the unconditioned knowledge of the absolute, it must in its way ask the question of inception. Even though this question must keep entirely to the domain of subjectity, the knowledge of the un-provability and prior-certainty of the absolute is a sign of the inceptive. But what is nearer still, more immediate—that is, of a closeness that is essentially other—is beyng.

And we must learn to become, inwardly, this closest closeness, and to experience the clearing of being.

---

14. *Beiträge zur Philosophie (vom Ereignis)* (GA 65).
15. *Besinnung* (GA 66).
16. *Die Geschichte des Seyns* (GA 69).
17. *Metaphysik und Nihilismus* (GA 67).
18. *Zum Ereignis-Denken* (GA 73).

Up until now, though, the mistaking of the closeness of being has been still more abysmal than the undertaking of a man who first asks his neighbor whether the sun is shining. (*The Wandsbeck Messenger* knew and dearly loved this "shining.")

83. *From Inception*

—to what extent is onto-historical thinking, or the inquiring of the truth of beyng, itself the history *of* beyng?

Inasmuch as its word, from which all that is historiographical has fallen away, succeeds in becoming pure saying, because it says creatively the stillness, and bestows the gift of beyng into steadfastness.

Inasmuch as the word of beyng is here the voicing of the attunement of pure giving, the truth "of" beyng unfolds and is its history.

84. *The Relation to Being*

must not be considered like the relation to beings. And anyway, must not every relating to . . . already in its very character cover over that which is related-to?

Thought from out of being, do we even ask correctly when we start off on the track of talking about the relation to being? Doesn't this already go astray? And why?

85. From Inception

In the inception, being announces itself; here, the thinking of being confronts the differentiation into what- and that- being.

Therefore it also cannot be said that only "existence" is thought inceptively, because the what-question remains undeveloped. "Existence" is first grasped solely in resistance to ἰδέα and as οὐσία. φύσις–ἀλήθεια; ἕν; λόγος say the inceptive: inception, *emergence itself*:

not: that beings are;

not: what beings are—

rather: being unfolds—being "is."

The projection "of" being.

The casting-off "of" being.

The thrownness of being-there.

The projective throw of beings.

The casting and the more inceptive inception.

The casting and φύσις.

The casting and the event.

86. Dialogue in the Inception

How the first inception speaks *to* the more inceptive inception, how it addresses it, but also how this latter lets the first unfold more inceptively.

How far this dialogue is the word of beyng as the *history* of beyng.

That, in the historical, intervals of time disappear, but without letting anything arise that is extra-temporal in itself.

How, in the inception, being is concealment, and how concealment also attunes [*be-stimmt*] the more inceptive.

87. Inception

Here there is no commencement *of* something, within or for an ordered succession.
Inception is not some kind of raising-up of something into what it properly is.
The inception is itself the *unfolding of being*—this *is* inception.

"Inception" also more original than ἀρχή—when by this is meant only a means and a conceptualizing of the interpretation of origin.

88. Inception and the Distinctive Mark of Western History

The "*Western*" is itself inceptively determined, in that, in the early Greek domain, being as truth came to emergence and truth advanced away into the essence of τέχνη. Today, the entire planet is Western, however much China and India may still prove to be old "cultures."

The "Western" is not geographical, nor its subsequent expansion, but is rather historical, this historicality being meant inceptively.

The singularity of this inception is the ground of the comprehensiveness of the domination of that which corresponds to this inception as advancing-away and is metaphysics and its completion.

How far "Americanism" is the appropriate form of planetarism.

Planetarism is the turning away of the inception into the non-essence of its advancing-away—

being as power; power as machination.

Inceptive thinking is that thinking that is attuned from the inception, determined by the incipience of inception.

89. Onto-Historical Thinking
(Fundamental Traits)

is above all the inquiring naming of beyng (*is* beyng?), and steadfast insistence in the being-there that is first indicated there.

Onto-historical thinking is the oneness of the original inkling of the other inception and the recollecting of the first inception.

In this reciprocal inceptuality, thinking is the placing into confrontation of the inceptions, of their essential consequences (metaphysics) and their preparation (*Overcoming of Metaphysics*).[19]

This thinking (which, thus, is inceptive) is interpretation, because it has a relation to history, and here, history is the appropriative event of the truth of beyng.

The thinking of the first inception does not know itself as such but rather has its inceptuality in the pure saying of being: ἔστιν γὰρ εἶναι.

Only out of the inceptive thinking that thinks into the other inception does knowledge of beyng itself come into inceptuality and thus into historicality. But, from now on, recollecting and hinting must equally be an inquiring: Is there beyng?

90. Inceptive Thinking in the
Crossing into the Other Inception

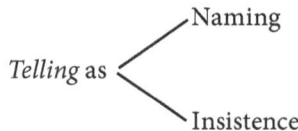

$$
\textit{Telling as} \begin{cases} \text{Naming} \\ \text{Insistence} \end{cases}
$$

(cf. *Overcoming*;[20] The Abandonment of the Differentiation
and the Still-Allowing of Beings)

---

19. *Metaphysik und Nihilismus* (GA 67).
20. Ibid.

1. Inceptively transitional thinking is just the naming of more inceptive beyng (appropriative event—concealment), but this naming never and nowhere appears as an effecting or an influencing. It is never "knowledge." It is never "science." Above all it is not merely symbolic. The naming is inceptive knowing, spoken of beyng itself, such that the telling (cf. *Telling*)[21] remains attuned as the word of beyng.

2. Above all, though, inceptively transitional thinking is the steadfast insistence in being-there. Being-there is the essential ground, appropriated from beyng, of the truth of beyng's capacity to be grounded in a humanity.

   Steadfast insistence is not able to displace the human into being-there. This casting of thrownness into being-there comes always from the projective throw of beyng itself as event.

   But, in the naming, there must certainly have been an inkling: clues toward the practice of insistent thoughtful reflection.

   What is first, and that which all steadfast insistence must make ready, is the listening submission to beyng. And to begin with this can occur transitionally in the naming and unfolding of the differentiation (cf. Summer Semester 1941).[22]

   Such guiding-words about beyng can never, though, prepare "lived-experience"; rather, the hearing of the word requires abandoning all experience-craving, and subjectity along with it.

   How, though, should steadfast insistence be achieved? Through a saying of the inter-venings of beyng into beings.

3. Inceptive thinking, as recollective hinting, is the confrontation of first and other inceptions.

4. Inceptive thinking, as the thinking of beyng as inception, is essentially *onto-historical*. (Bearing in mind that in truth this name says the same thing twice.)

5. Inceptive thinking is interpretive. Interpretation is of history as the history of beyng, and is related only to this (cf. Remarks on Interpreting).[23]

---

21. *Zum Wesen der Sprache und Zur Frage nach der Kunst* (GA 74).
22. *Grundbegriffe* (GA 51).
23. *Zum Wesen der Sprache und Zur Frage nach der Kunst* (GA 74), 156.

91. The More Inceptive Questioning
(The Inquiring)

asks: *Is there beyng*? And out of this, the differentiation-abandoning question overcomes the guiding-question of metaphysics: "What is a being?"

More inceptive than the what-question is the is-question, namely, the one that emerges from beyng itself. This question does not wish to declare beyng a being; rather, the question promises beyng, questioningly, to beyng, such that *beyng be only its beyng* [*das Seyn dem Seyn einzig das Seine sei*].

But, at the same time, the historicality of beyng lies within this more inceptive is-question—the saying of inceptuality—without its being decided by the questioners *that* beyng is; because this is the proper domain only of inception itself. Thus the question: Is there beyng? has rather more the meaning: whether the questioners are and are prepared for steadfast insistence in the truth of the event.

If, in essence, only beyng is, such indeed that it never becomes a being (of which alone we ordinarily say it "is"), then what does this common way of speaking mean: beings are?

92. The Leap
(The incepting from out of the inception)
(The inception is into the inception)

Being can be arrived at from no being, because then it would already be projected being, unknown in its thrownness, just given out of "hand."

Every attempt to come to beyng along such a way, which is the way of metaphysics, is deception and semblance.

This semblance is essentially more abyssal than that which Kant pointed to as "dialectic."

But this semblance must arise from beyng. Why? Because it is not "nothing"?

Thus, thought through in a sufficiently essential way, precisely *this* semblance gives an inkling of beyng.

How is the inkling to be taken, and how should we pursue it? The leap.
That thinking thinks out of beyng.
But how? Being-there.

93. *The Inceptiveness of Inception*

Beyng—essential unfolding—telling
The un-said
The keeping-silent—
arising out of the self-concealing of concealment.

Inception

Inceptive thinking accepts what is to be thought only from this itself—that is, from being.

Being must project itself *toward* thinking. Thinking must be carried away in this projecting-toward and must itself thus become the projectively thrown [*Ent-werfenden*].

The unsaid not brought into word, either because left essentially undecided, or because decided and arriving thus at the ungroundedness of essence, or else decided, and thus *a questionlessness* laid as the ground.

Plato's unsaid of the third kind: the essence of truth decided—oriented toward ἰδέα!

But this unsaid only to be really experienced:

1. When the first inception made knowable.
2. When, above all in the other inception, the confrontation is arrived at, and out of this the essence of truth as essential unfolding of being, and in various different ways.

What is properly to be thought can remain unsaid because it is in essence still left undecided, but also because it was decided in such a way that it either points off into the ungrounded or is diffused into a questionlessness.

94. *The Thinking Ahead into Inception*

must pass through a series of decisions in order that "inception" be taken in the first place as historiographical and thought as Greco-Roman antiquity.

Here arise questions as to whether "antiquity" was experienced and conceived:

1. "Humanistically" (in all possible variants) or "classically," whereby both are joined together.
2. Whether Greek (from out of the being of beings) or Roman (from the domination of the human over beings).
3. If Greek, though, whether Platonically or inceptively.
4. If inceptively, whether the inception is thought only as that which precedes Plato and is seen looking backward from him, or whether inception is thought inceptively, and the "Platonic" thus thought, not as "consummation" in the sense of "fulfillment," but rather as a flowing-out.
5. If inception is thought inceptively, whether, in addition, the most extreme, the singular, is risked: the other inception, or whether it is just some former strangeness that is acknowledged and invoked.
6. If the most extreme is risked, whether, in addition, *thoughtful reflection* is undertaken or whether a hasty result is expected.

95. *Claim and Response* ("Claim" and Result) The Telling[24]

The claim, that the essence of the human is summoned through the word of beyng.

Thus Claimed, the *essence* of the human is directed along the path toward insisting in beyng, which says: this steadfastness unfolds itself in its own freedom, as *the* knowledge.

---

24. Ibid.

This steadfastness opens the ground for previously concealed Dasein (non-essencing).

Such is the creative unfolding of being-there and the essence of the response to the word of beyng.

All this eventuates; it "is" beyng itself. Only from the appropriative event spring the "claim-sayings" [*An-sprüche*] in which man establishes his essence and thus himself. What they can accomplish, and how this must be accomplished, is decided already from out of beyng.

"Freedom"

The human's highest claim is now a claimlessness: it no longer needs "claims"; it does not need to "make" them because its essence is in the richness of the essential destitution of beyng.

This is grounded in the proper domain, the belongingness to beyng that arises in the appropriative event.

Thus, there is a release of the human into being-there, as the abyss of stewardship along the way to beyng.

Freedom is neither just freedom from, nor freedom to, nor spontaneity, nor the possibility of good and evil; rather, it is the displacement into the confrontation of beings with beyng; it is release into the belongingness to beyng.

Freedom is the release into the race with sheltering, self-concealing beyng, for the essential transformation of the human into Dasein.

All is essential unfolding of beyng; from this, as appropriative event, the essence of history is determined.

It unfetters the wildness and prepares the mildness; the belonging-together of both is the trajectory for the path, which as way and step achieves the grounding of appropriation.

Freedom—is release of the essence of the human.

Release is the steadfastness in being-there.

Steadfastness is taken over in a *human* way in the stewardship of thoughtful reflection.

Release unfolds as assignment into belonging to the truth of beyng.

Freeing-release [*Be-freiung*] is the essential of beyng as claim, which steadfastness addresses upon arising, the arising-from consisting in pursuing the essential transformation of man appropriated from beyng.

Freedom as release is a projective casting of expectancy onto the carrying-out of the confrontation of beings with being.

96. Inception and the Simple

The simple is neither facile, nor empty, nor meager, nor fleeting.

The simple is the receptacle of the singular—of the essential unfolding of beyng. So long as we cling to beings and explain and calculate from there, we never arrive at the simplicity of beyng.

Thoughtful reflection into beyng as the way to simplicity.

As receptacle, it is the sheltering of beyng in the appropriative event—inception.

III. Event and Being-there

A. The Event

97. Event and Beings
(Cf. the Difference and the Differentiation)

If beings are eventally appropriated, that is, when they are conveyed into the unconcealment of the clearing of the there, this does not just mean that "beings" now come into consciousness and, as the beings that they are, become objective. For in this way they never *are* beings. "Being-ness" eventuates along with the appropriative event.

That beings come into the open also does not say just that they engage the possibility of objectification; rather, it says that they come into being—and into telling and into word. But telling and word are not expression and setting but are rather the essential unfolding of being.

The rose blooms in the poem of the poet and only there; but this "blooming" is not simply said retrospectively of a supposedly real thing, a being; rather, it alone is the being. But this is also why, in accordance with the uniqueness and rarity of being, originative poetizing is rare. Roses bloom but rarely.

But for much of mankind, sunk as it is into the comprehensible, things are simply objectively present and capable of being secured; indeed, even this "leaving being be" is one way in which beings are given over to being.

The "assigning"[1] claims the human. But this mark of the human is not grounded in his subjicity. That, in metaphysics, the human is both the proper being and the fundamental image of the same—as microcosm (cf. the question of anthropomorphism)[2]: this is what grounds this distinguishing mark in the giving over into being and is thus how the human is conjoined, through being, to its stewardship.

In all that first begins in the other inception, obtains all that, in metaphysics, was truth; not, though, as dialectical sublation, but as a more inceptive determination. *Oblivious of the event*, subjicity arises through the appropriative eventuation of a claiming of the human for being, through being.

---

1. What is meant is appropriative adoption [*An-eignung*], properly understood as the inceptively seizing appropriation [*An-fangende Eignung*] into ownness, but not the evental appropriating into the twisting-free of beyng into the parting.
2. *Die Metaphsik des deutschen Idealismus* (GA 49), edited by G. Seubold (Frankfurt am Main: Vittorio Klostermann, 1991).

If we think beings themselves in their domain, inceptively and onto-historically, then it is just as erroneous to dream up beings-in-themselves as it is to declare that beings are given only for a consciousness. In both cases the truth-character of being is not thought inceptively, and so beings are either, once again, kept from the openness (within the same) and independent, or else are simply explained through consciousness (in the sense of representedness).

But if, just once, beings were to be experienced and preserved in being (as appropriative event), then what would also be revealed is just how far the attunement of being-there is tuned from out of the human, but also how far it lies enclosed in beings themselves. For beings, being is not just a covering of brightness that glides across "beings" from time to time.

Being neither the making nor the effecting of beings.

Being neither objectifying-representing beings.

Being neither covering-over—

Rather, being, as appropriative eventuation, is the giving-over into being of non-beings or of beings abandoned by being. This is how beings themselves become emergent, and in emergence (φύσις, thought now more inceptively) rise-up into a lingering.

Everything that is essentially given to being brings beings themselves, in so far as they "are," into what is in each case granted to them.

The claim of beings—that they have the essence of being at their disposal and explain being from themselves as *their* determination—has become so ossified through metaphysics that any attempt to say being itself as telling is always caught up in metaphysics, is concocted after its fashion and brought down by its calculus.[3]

But being is not the translation of beings (i.e., of the "world") into the interiority of the human being, conceived thus out of I-ness because already posited as representing subjectity.

If we were to take up a counterposition, here, where what matters is the crossing into the other inception, it would be better to say: not the translation into the interiority of the human being, but rather the transformation of the essence of the human through appropriation into being as event.

Beings are deposed from their priority and yet are not thereby dispersed into being, quite the opposite: they are more being-like than before.[4]

Beings can neither take refuge in subjectity (in any kind of "sublimation" through "the spiritual"), nor are they reduced to a mere μὴ ὄν; nor, equally, is the "being" of beings only a "fiction" contrived by beings themselves.

For the human is not subject; being is not ὄν as ὄντως ὄν in the sense of ἰδέα; a being cannot be explained from out of the "becoming" that it indeed already "is."

---

3. (Where has such an attempt ever been risked?)

4. (That which is propriated into its ownness).

Being is also *still* not a being such that, in being, a being would be doubled; rather, in being, a being is singular occasion, looming up into the singularity of being. But the looming is different each time, according to whether the being that is propriated to being [*an-geeignet*] is as stone, as tree, as animal, as human, or as god.

The looming up as the being-in-being [*Seiendsein*] of beings in the event. Looming up is not representedness and is no mere appearing; looming up is emergence but, at the same time, a staying-back in the beingless.

Looming up—as a coming forth and towering up into the clearing, is also no mere lighting-up but is, rather, inceptive and always singular.

In the appropriative event beings are not changed into being as the interiority of the "I." The intimacy of being is far from any human emotionality.

Rather, beings are changed, from their sometime beinglessness into the exteriorization of the looming up, into the incursion of the inter-vening and its sustaining.

B. Event and Dis-appropriation

98. The Beingless and Beings Dis-appropriation

Only in the truth of being can both be experienced. But how do they themselves unfold, and what is meant, here, by this "unfolding"? A being *is* not—as *beingless,* but therefore it is also not "nothing."

It can neither be said that the beingless is, nor that it is not.

But because being comes to intervene into the beingless and, as inception, incepts beings, therefore beings are, in a certain way, "prior to" and older than being—namely, as the beingless that subsequently comes into being. Beings are the "a priori" of being, provided confusion does not arise here through the use of metaphysical labels for being and for the in-being beings [*seiende Seiende*] that unfold beyond all metaphysics.

Beinglessness, though, does not mean the abandonment of beings by being; because in the abandonment by being, beings are indeed in-being, only in such a way that they appear to be uniquely themselves without needing being.

In being's abandonment, beings are left to themselves and take on the appearance of not needing being.

In beinglessness beings are neither in-being nor not in-being.

The abandonment by being is an essential unfolding of being itself, the event of the unleashing of beings into machination.

Although beinglessness is still conceived from being, it does not arise from being, inasmuch as the beingless does not need being.

However, in beinglessness something most extreme about the essence of being can be grasped (inception—receding—parting).

Here—in "beinglessness" and in the "beingless"—is a demand, within which no metaphysics finds its way, but where the courage of onto-historical thinking can find attunement and where, at the same time, the uniqueness of being can eventuate in its rareness.

In being's abandonment (i.e., the machination of beings), beings are wholly outside beinglessness.

The beingless is beyond the nothing, because in the nothing beings are already in being and are in the first place only non-beings.

But the beingless is also essentially other and more than non-being; it is beings themselves, the not—that beings (i.e., as eventally appropriated) are.

Beinglessness is the *disappropriation* of beings—but disappropriation is not simply nihilation, for it is more essential and more inceptive than mere nihilation and destruction.

Disappropriation lets "stand" in the being-less.

But what does "standing" mean—constancy?

And letting-stand and beinglessness—do these not still, as disappropriation, belong to the event?

Such that disappropriation *is* only in the event.

Or is disappropriation the event as parting, and is the leave-taking still also that of disappropriation—?

In comparison with all this, the thought of the "nothing" is a harmless, easy one—a dependable metaphysical essence.

The beingless "is" the pre-inceptive and post-inceptive, not insofar as it has the character of inception, but rather in that it "becomes" [*wird*] a being only in inception and dis-integrates [*entwird*] in receding.

The beingless is knowable only in being and knowable only in the manner of an "essence."

But here the innermost nihilating of being itself first reveals itself: that it is not in itself only concealment and refusal but rather, as receding, is disappropriation.

Disappropriation is the ultimacy of the intimacy of refusal; it is the parting, not only of beings, but the parting of their own essence.

From out of the beingless, then, a sharpened glimpse is afforded into the essential unfolding of being and of inception.

Yet what does this mean for humanity and for divinity? The event of disappropriation?

That everything is thus essentially in being, and is thus untouchable by any annihilation of beings and by their devastation. Because we have for so long and so blindly hung onto the beings of metaphysics that the beingless and the parting seem to us precisely that which we have to block as soon as possible; for nihilism certainly seems, now, to be overflowing into infinity.

And yet, here, uniquely and for the first time, the uniqueness of being begins, its uncommonness not limiting its singularity but, rather, un-limiting into the pure essence of receding as the fulfillment of inception.

99. [Beings] as the Beingless

That which the thinkable resists in essence, and that which a thinking in beings does not permit, must be thought here.

How far, and under what conditions can we still place ourselves into this greatest extremity of the thought of being?

When beings "are" the beingless, only then do we arrive at the determination that is always and again sought when we take the being in-and-through-themselves of beings to be what is most proper to beings. The beingless does not need being and "is" nevertheless not the nihilated.

Does being, though, in this way not become a mere covering-over of beings? No.

Everything depends on whether we think the essential unfolding of being inceptively enough.[5]

---

5. The essential unfolding is the event as the turn of the assignment of transforming affinity [Verwandtnis] and of the giving over of the twisting-free.

C. Being-there

(Disposition)

Attunement

—

Human   *Gods*

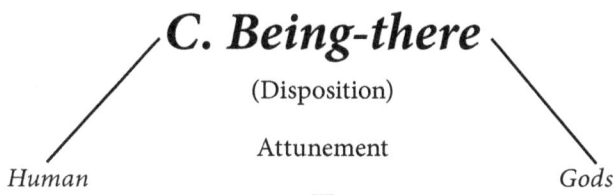

100. Being-there

To "think" above all from out of the abruptness of inception: out of being ("-be-ing"), out of unconcealment (-there), and out of the appropriative eventuation of the human that is steadfast in being-there, grounding it in beings.

Being-there, above all, from "being" and from the "human," to think being as inception,
but the human as the sacrifice that is belonging in the event.

This is why the first attempts, in *Being and Time*, to think being-there are continuously thrown back and forth between an interpretation of the human being (though not an anthropology) and inquiring after the truth of being (no longer metaphysics, knowing being only as making-possible and as *a priori*).

*

Being-there tends the essence of the truth of beyng.

It is the essential tending of all that is essential and is thus never beyng itself in its incipience but, rather, only what is appropriated.

The *essential tending of beyng* is attainable only for and through the thinking of beyng itself.

101. Being-there and Vibrance

The essence of the human, then, is only essentially determined when "essence" is thought exclusively, and in an essentially fitting way, as being, and human being itself thought creatively out of the relation of beyng itself to the human. This creative thinking of the human being leads into domains closed to all metaphysics, which in its obstinacy is anyway sealed off from these. These domains, though, are still veiled in the first inception, because it is in emerging as unconcealment that being first essences and first claims the human as the lingering in unconcealment, though directing him right away toward beings, which offer themselves to him as ζωή; the "life" within which it is λόγος that is objectively present and that supports the "human."

But before it brings into play a determination of the human, the relation of beyng to the human already conceals in itself the appropriative eventuation of the clearing of the there that unfolds as being-there. Amid this singular and inceptive openness of all that is open (i.e., that is unconcealed in accord with being), the essence of the human vibrates, provided it is appropriated into the relation to being by being itself. The human is not the "human" in it additionally happens upon the relation to being. But on the other hand, this relation to being is also not only the relationship of the human to beings. The relation of being to the human is the event of the grounding of "being-in-the-world" that, for its part, already lets the relating to beings unfold.

Talk of the relation of beyng to the human is always problematic, in so far as it takes "the human" as something decided and determined in advance; whereas, what the discourse means is that it is beyng that first draws the human into relation [*einbezieht in den Bezug*], thus first initiating him into and detaining him [*erzieht und hinzieht*] in humanness.

The essence of the human, which is thought here only historically, that is, explicitly or implicitly in view of this relation, vibrates in its relation to beyng.

This vibrancy means the undecided plenitude of what is decidable through the human's own standing-within being-there.

What thinking names inceptively as "νοῦς," and as *mens* and "spirit" (reason) is already a kind of capacity, from out of which the human holds itself in vibration, without itself being able to appropriate this in an essentially inceptive way. Instead, the allotment of the human to being is immediately shifted into its relating to beings, a relating through which "being" is also then accepted, as κοινόν.

Every anthropology, even the "existentiell," which retrieves "spirit," opposing it to "life" and recognizing in the play of this opposition the fundamental trait of the human, remains closed off from the inceptive thinking of the vibrancy.

The human being vibrates in beyng, provided not only that it is differentiated from other beings as the being that it is, and indeed as a being, but also that it is in its essence displaced and thrown into the differentiation of being over against beings. The turning toward beings is always this and that, one and not the other; turnings toward beings are neither caused by beings nor are they produced by the human; they are vibrated-through by beyng into the essential unfolding in-the-midst that is at the same time the clearing in which all beings emerge. This means: beyng already determines the non-human being and at the same time determines the human being in oppositional vibrancy and, in vibration's midst, determines the relationship of the human to beings and their incursion into the human.

This oscillation is not to be thought "mechanically": what it means is that being first lifts beings into the open of the openness of being and bears them in such a lifting. The bearing in the back and forth of the lifting is the vibrancy. And the bearing up of the human being does not originate from a sinking of a soul into a body. The bearing up is the vibrancy from the momentum of the thrownness out of the projective casting into which beyng eventually appropriates the human being, toward the grounding of a stewardship of the truth of beyng.

102. *Being and the Human*
(Cf. Summer Semester 1941 Guiding
Words on Beyng[6]
Cf. The Remoteness of the Inception[7])

Does a distinctive connectedness of being to the human hold sway from out of and in inception? Is the human the guardian, appropriated into being-there, of the truth of beyng?

And why, and to what extent? Because he has the possibility of steadfastness in being-there and, before that, ratio, λόγος, νοῦς—

---

6. *Grundbegriffe* (GA 51).
7. Ibid., 11.

But how does he have this possibility? The fact that he has this, is already event—inceptuality.

This "the fact that" does not mean ascertaining an objective aptitude of a discoverable living creature.

This "the fact that"—is the beckoning of beyng into the inception.

"The human" must no longer in the first place be animal or even ζῷον λόγον ἔχον—[8]; instead, the human must, at once, sacrifice its belonging to inception in its suddenness. But whence this *must*? From the singularity of beyng.

Beyng never unfolds at the behest of the human; the human is, at most, at the behest of beyng. But this never means "because of" beyng; it means at the behest of so that the human, as itself, attains its essence.

Being is a happen-stance for the human; the appropriation into beyng does not depend on the human, and it also does not attest to any lack in beyng, as opposed to the human—as if being might need the human.

But when being unfolds in its truth and when this, as the inter-vening, eventuates beings, then the human has its distinctive determination toward the grounding of the truth of being in beings; and thence, in the aspect of non-essence, comes the possibility of presumption and of the domain of the overman.

(cf. Nietzsche's Metaphysics[9])

103. Being-there
(cf. Inception and Truth)

is the appropriative eventuation of the grounding of the essential unfolding of truth in the domain of the human, so long as truth unfolds as the unconcealing concealment in which the incipience of inception recedes into itself.

Admittedly, it seems at first as if only "accord" with beings would make it possible to leave beings to themselves and by themselves. And yet the *adaequatio* of representing is precisely the hidden mode of intrusiveness of the human, through which he delivers up beings to himself, but without thinking being inceptively. Indeed, representing appears to achieve a self-opening, and yet it is *this*

---

8. Unless we think ζῷον aletheically.

9. *Nietzsche* (GA 6.2), 231–300.

that is closed off to the clearing of being, refusing the unleashing of beings into being.

Representing cannot appropriate the event of being as inter-vening.

The letting-be of being, and not only of beings, alone makes possible being-there and steadfastness within it.

104. Being-there

Being-there is the response [*Erwiderung*] to beyng, the countering-response [*Er-widerung*] that beyng itself eventuates appropriatively. It is not beings that make possible the encounter with beyng, in other words the belonging to beyng in its pure safeguarding.

Here, countering-response means the encountering of the projecting into the clearing opened by the projection. Proper to the response is the bringing forth of the proper domain of the event; yet the "there" must *be* [*seyn*], when inception crosses into receding incipience and the concealment of its essence comes, resisting, to unconcealment.

For the human being, being-there can be taken up only in steadfastness in the parting. Inception here eventuates an acknowledgment of beyng, which would lose everything that gives it essential hold if it were to rely on public dissemination and thereafter allow itself to be in the least evaluated.

Being-there is the appropriately eventuated site that precedes the crossing of inception, a site that is attuned to the stillness that only the dignity of beyng is capable of safeguarding.

Neither the public sphere of the multitude nor even the selectivity of the few suffices for the steadfastness in the stillness. The telling of beyng must remain in namelessness; it eventuates, as if it were never eventuated.

Only remoteness in the stillness of being-there responds to being as the parting, in which inception is intercepted in its dignity.

105. Being-there

unfolds only in the other inception and remains *incomparable* with anything previously recognized or achieved by metaphysics as the essential configuration of the human (soul, spirit, consciousness, self-consciousness, reason, life). It is incomparable, not just because being-there is some other determination of the human. In the proper sense it is not this at all: rather, being-there *is* only as essential consequence, and not merely as alternative content (e.g., "Dasein" instead of subjectity). It is in another mode and in another essence, before the other inception. Its essence belongs entirely to beyng, as the appropriative event that the other inception is. "Being-there" cannot be elucidated by analogy and can be nowhere accommodated within familiar frameworks. It *itself* alone determines the locational and temporal occasion [*Ort- und Zeit-schaft*] of the grounding of the truth of being into beings.

The highest granting, eventuating as beyng, is that of being-there.

Being-there, understood in the entirely other sense of *Being and Time* but thought, as here, *still more* inceptively, is the essential unfolding of space-time for all being of beings.

What is named "being-there" remains alien to all metaphysical thinking but is also not to be accommodated within that which unfolds in the first inception.

Above all, the current appearance of a connection with the human is to be fended off—an appearance to which, in a certain respect, *Being and Time* still fell victim, and that maintains its hold even where the correspondingly transformed *essence* of historical man is claimed from beyng for being-there.

In the twisting-free of beyng, being-there is precisely unleashed and released into its inceptuality.

106. Being-there

is in its essence inaccessible to all metaphysics.

But is also not to be experienced in its singular role, which has no similarity to the structure of the truth of beings and is not met with or accommodated to an arrangement of world, human, god, and so forth; for being-there is before all else never the same as the human.

107. Being-there

and the thrownness into the limits of unconcealment and concealment.
Thrownness as the essential unfolding of the history of being-there.

108. Being-there and the Human

Essential origin of the human, insofar as the latter is experienced from its rela-
tion to being, a relation that unfolds only in the character of an inclusion of the
human in beyng, "through" beyng.
Being
Appropriative event (of being-there)
Attuning (word of beyng—concealment—keeping silent)
Attunement
Im-position
Disposition
Steadfastness
Situatedness (corporeality)
> (Conceived otherwise than in *Being and Time*, where equated with at-
> tunement)

Being-there, as dispositional fortitude [*Ge-müt*], is attunedness through the
attuning of beyng—;

Being-there unfolds as the pure re-sonance [*Wieder-klang*] of beyng; being-
there never transforms being into itself but, rather, insists in being given over to
the inter-vening.

109. The Other Inception
Humanity–
Divinity–

is the appropriative event, and transforms the essence of the human and above all that of the gods. Not merely to make other gods appear in place of the old; rather, the essence of divinity is other.

Humanity, in the other inception, unfolds in the safeguarding of the truth of beyng, in order to vouchsafe its twisting-free.

Divinity, in the other inception, stems from the proper domain of the beyng of truth, that is, from the receding essence of inception (the "last god" is the god of incipience).

Just as the human is no longer *animal rationale*, so, too, has God thrown off his metaphysical demiurgic essence.

The innermost non-essentiality of Christianity (as metaphysics and cultural claim) lies in its inability to allow a repudiation of God through being, even though the lamentable state of the Christian God for the slightest thoughtful reflection in the face of world-atrocity, which is always in one way or another justified in his name, has become clear.

Humanity and divinity correspond to one another only in being-there, which is already the appropriative eventuation of the event.

110. Divinity in the Other Inception

The other inception is more inceptive and, therefore, begins expressly from and toward its receding.

We intimate the god of sheltering.

We intimate the goddess of receding.

We do not know the history of this divinity.

111. Event, Ownness, Destitution

The highest ownness of humanity that is prepared, following the overcoming of metaphysics, for steadfastness in being-there, thus accepting the grounding of the truth of beyng and entering into its history, is, as a result of this entry into the event, *destitution*.

Destitution, here, does not indicate lack but rather steadfastness (disposition, attunedness) in the simple and singular: but this is the essential unfolding of beyng.

From this, beings first stand forth inceptively into the clearing of the there.

Destitution and bestowal—

Letting-be in the essential unfolding of appropriative eventuation.

112. Being-there and Attunement

Attunement attunes as attuning voice—as word, that is, as keeping silent, as being.

Attunement in being-there—is to be grasped through no anthropological or psychological capacity and in no domain (body—soul—spirit).

Attunement and the essential unfolding of truth.

Attunement and the attuning of the history of beyng.

Attunement not only in terms of Dasein, indeed, in truth, not at all; (therefore disposition). Attunement as essential unfolding of beyng.

Metaphysics and its self-understanding coerces one into the view that "attunement" would be graspable only as psychological, moralistic, anthropological.

113. Attunements and Beyng

Proceeding anthropologically, all kinds of "attunements" can be discovered, and thus, a botany, or an herbarium, of attunements can be established, according to which one attunement can be endorsed and others discarded, depending on the attunement and in keeping with the wishes of the "time."

But because all anthropology belongs to metaphysics and, for metaphysics, the truth of being cannot even come into question, therefore the essential relation of being to attunement remains concealed. But this relation is the only one that a thinker can think in relation to attunements and their essence.

It is immediately apparent that "attunements" in their multiplicity are not lying ready like hiding-places for whatever feeling-states the human undergoes. On the contrary, attunements are in each case an essence unified out of the historical essence of being. All attunements accord in the essence of being, and their opposition is only an appearance produced by a constricting of the essence of attunement, there where it affects to be pouring out its riches.

The Fundamental Attunement of Thankfulness

114. Attunement

To think its essence can only mean listening thoughtfully to the attunement of the attuning.

But not composing treatises on kinds of attunements in general, as if they were objects present at hand.

Steadfastness in attunement is first necessary and essential in the sustaining of the crossing to the other inception.

Here, appropriative eventuation, and with it, the attuning of the attuning voice, has begun.

But *the attunement of the crossing* is:

The courageous generosity of patience in destitution [Die Großmut der Langmut in der Armut], *from out of the richness of the appropriative eventuation of Dasein, through the intimacy of the more inceptive first inception.*

115. "Anxiety"

If one sees anxiety only as "fearfulness," putting it about as a timidity, this arouses the suspicion that this kind of minimizing of anxiety is an attempt to evade it. Thus, what would be in play would be an "anxiety" (in other words, a fear) of anxiety. And, in fact, that is the main obstacle: that the "heroic" presentation of all behaviors leads to mistaking anxiety in essence and not experiencing its fundamental trait as a generosity.

Essentially (which means grasped from out of the relation to beyng), what holds sway in anxiety is awe before beyng, and acknowledgment.

But thus conceived, anxiety is distinguished by letting the not-ness of beyng itself be attunedly determined.

116. Beyng—Being-there—Disposition

is the courage [*Mut*] of the disposition [*Gemüt*]. In the disposition, every courage, every imposing demand and every impression has gathered itself originally.

The disposition emboldens and discourages, makes demands for and from.

The disposition is attunedness through the attunement of the attuning of beyng. The disposition is being-there. How beyng itself attunes and how the disposition of being-there imposes itself.

The disposition unconceals and conceals, stands insistent in the midst of the clearing of beyng.

Indigence	and	the plenitude of beyng as event
Gentleness	and	the stillness of beyng
Patience	and	the whiling
Grace	and	this threefold courage as resplendence of inception (generosity of patience for the dignity of the destitution of appropriative eventuation)
Generosity	and	beyng as concealment (dignity)
Melancholy	and	the abyssality of beyng
Equanimity	and	the ambivalence of beyng
Resentment and discontent	and	the non-essence of beyng

117. Awe

Nietzsche says: "the *great* human being is lacking and, *in consequence, awe.*"[10] (Zarathustra)

This "in consequence" expresses the essence of modern metaphysics and testifies to the forgetfulness of being and to the delusion of producing an essentiality of the human through the great human.

Here, the question of what "great" might mean can be passed over.

Instead we must consider that awe unfolds as dispositional attunement in relation to being itself and that, without this relation, it remains only incidental for the human animal, and thus is as insignificant as any change to its skin and hair.

Even if we were to attempt, reasonably enough, to simply invert the sentence, it would still not hit on the essential. The sentence would then mean only: "awe is lacking and, as a consequence, the great human being." As far as it goes, this sentence does give a hint, as it shows that there must first be openness for what is essential, in order that a greatness—and then perhaps also a great human being—be appreciated and recognized.

But what does this "awe is lacking" say? Is it only the identification of a lacuna in the sphere of dispositional attunements? Or is this a historical word that, suspecting nothing of the human forgetfulness of being, and in consequence of having been long excluded from an essential position, says the acknowledgment of beyng?

Awe is lacking: the human loses its way in the abandonment of being.

118. *The History of the Human*

If one wanted to ask directly how inceptive thinking, that is, onto-historical thinking, might think the future situation of the human: what shape it might grant to the human amid beings, and what "order" of beings themselves might

---

10. Friedrich Nietzsche, "Nachgelassene Fragmente, 1884–85," in *Nietzsches Werke: Kritische Gesamtausgabe*, 7.3, edited by G. Colli and M. Montinari (Berlin: De Gruyter, 1974), 77.

result, then this question might indeed be considered very "interesting," but no more than this. It attests right away to being yet again minded to skip over beyng in favor of beings, seeing as "oneself" and the human has anyway been established amid beings. The constancy of the human in the world is settled in advance as decided, and everything must aim at the securing of the same. Amid all this fretting, one is thinking, unawares, in old modes: metaphysically-humanistically, and not shying away from construing this question of "humanity" back into the inception of Western history, into the domain of the Greeks, even as its sole concern.

One other offshoot of this metaphysical humanism—and only an offshoot—is biologism, which invokes the advancement of the procreation of life and "thinks" about the human, seen as "eternal" "people." It is altogether quite lavish with the "eternity" of continued existence and with human "goals," without being troubled about the justification for these dicta and without first even considering the one thing: that these all derive from the forgetfulness of being, which grants all "power" to beings as the real and effective. Within this domain one busies oneself anew with some other or some former (and now restored) order of things, and with saving the human. What the truth of beyng demands for itself is entirely overlooked. Beyng as event neither demands nor encourages the passivity of the human. Steadfastness in the truth of beyng does not imply a "quietism," any more than it does an activism.

Beyng assigns into preparedness for the transformation of the essence of the human, and this means of its relation to beyng. And here, what comes to an abrupt end is any calculation and planning that has always already made sure in advance of beings in their *kind* of being.

Here is the essentially incalculable singularity of inception, which eventuates beyond calculation.

But history must still go on; something must happen to the human. Humanity must thus be given something to cling to, something in which it can understand itself. Again one talks as an "organizer" of the world and forgets two things: to begin with, one is failing to recognize that "history" "keeps moving" because it has in any case already long since been caught up in this process. And one fails to recognize that the knowledge of beyng, and steadfastness in this, is essentially a richness of the human, because it holds in readiness the undecidedness in which the human finds and grounds the essential, whence comes the nobility and the domain of sacrifice, as an inception and a uniqueness that shall be his.

The abuse of hopes and expectations in what is merely calculable and graspable, and the reduction to certainties and utilities have long since rendered humanity unreceptive to the unfolding of the simple and distant, of the noiseless and the succinct, and of that which needs yield no profit in order, as what is in-being [*als seiend*], to prove true.

119. The Human and Being as "Will"

Because the human holds within it the essential relation to being, being becomes manifest in the human and so, also, does the "will."

Otherwise, "will" is deemed a human capacity that would from thence be applied to the rest of beings.

In terms of the history of being, however, all is otherwise.

To know "will," "understanding," and the like, all as the dispositional fortitude of courage, and attunedness as the fundamental structure of *being-there*.

(cf. From the History of Being, 2.34)[11]

120. The Onto-Historical Essence of Death

Death—grasped from being-there and from steadfastness in it (that steadfastness that is determined as human being)—has the character of receding.

Death is assignment into what is most proper in the truth of being.

Death is assignment into the receding, is belongingness into inception.

Death—thought onto-historically—is never crossing into another "life," is not the conveying into a better permanence. Also not the illusion of survival in the human sense.

Death *is* receding, and that *is* the highest inception, *is* the most extreme concealment, *is* being.

Every anthropology stands clueless before death, and every theology is all too well-advised to be able to recognize its dignity in a singular question-worthiness.

---

11. *Nietzsche* (GA 6.2), 411–18.

D. Inter-venings
(Steadfast Insistence in Being-there)

121. Inter-venings

Inter-venings: that beyng as concealment, as unleashing into the abandonment of being, even as the admittance of machination, has inceptively incurred into beings.

Steadfast insistence must think ahead into humanity as being-there, and into its transformed essence.

The disposition and the impositions.

From this, right back again into the inceptuality of the attuning of the attunements.

122. Recollective Thinking-Ahead into the Inception

Inception is the essential unfolding of truth (the unconcealing concealment; in terms of the first inception: Ἀλήθεια).

The truth that thus unfolds *is* being. Being *is* as truth and it is this as inception.

In inception the plenitude of *event* first unfolds, which beyng initially names the other inception. Essential unfolding is itself incepting.

The thinking of inception, though, is no longer involved with beings; nor even with the differentiation, as if this might construct a bridge from beings to being.

In this, already acting contrary to *all* metaphysics (or better yet, beyond its persistent thinking), the dignity of the inceptuality of inception is established, even if initially everything still seems to stumble around in indeterminacy, and to be lost in "abstraction."

123. Inceptive Thinking

In the first inception, inceptuality is otherwise than in the other. In the first in-ception, the thinking of inception is so singularly absorbed by unconcealment [*Entborgenheit*] itself, so entirely engaged in its testimony (νοεῖν–λόγος), that unconcealment is not itself specifically acknowledged as the essential unfolding of being, that is, raised into inquiry. Unconcealment [*Unverborgenheit*] unfolds as what is first—what is unique—so singularly that concealing and concealment are never even thought of.

Because this does not happen, concealment is also withheld and does not de-termine the essential historicality of ἀλήθεια, hence the admitting into ὀρθότης.

First-inceptive thinking is letting-be [*Eingelassenheit*] into inception. Onto-historical thinking is recollection into the first inception as thinking-ahead into the other.

But even this onto-historical thinking never thinks "about" inception, as if statements "about" the essence of inception would be what is essential—; *pre-paredness for appropriative giving-over into the appropriative event is what is singular*. Moreover, recollective thinking-ahead is first of all transitional, and re-mains (through the attuning of beyng) singularly determined in this way; not in order to displace the dignity of being itself onto historical humanity but, rather, to provide an impulse, among the listening, toward thoughtful reflection on this dignity.

124. Onto-Historical Thinking as Inceptive

In the sense of the onto-historical dignifying of being itself as event, inceptive thinking is more inceptive.

Because it thinks into the intimacy of the abyssal grounding of inception, it thinks solely its oneness, thinking therefore at the same time the ultimate receding.

Onto-historical thinking is *receding* thinking. It thinks from out of the ulti-mate receding. Is it therefore destructive? On the contrary. It is destructive as the de-construction of metaphysics's burial of inception.

But the receding is highest in the singularity of inception.

(The onto-historical essence of human death is the giving-over into the receding of inception.)

(The intertwinement of the question of death with the unresolved question of being-there in *Being and Time* has this relation to its ground—still unknown, though intimated.)

*

The steadfast must have recognized the shattering of the gods within the overcoming of metaphysics. They must hope for nothing more from "gods." They linger over inception, even when the absolute is set up as God.

The steadfast must experience the lack of essence [*Wesenslosigkeit*] of *animal rationale* and must have overcome every anthropomorphizing, no longer deeming man to have created the gods. Because the creating, here, as much as the createdness of beings, is an ending—one that evades inception.

Inceptive dignity arises in beyng. Inceptive awe is the gracious demeanor of being-there.

125. Sheltering Concealment and Being-there/Impulse

What is the inceptive courage that provides the attunement that is attunedly determined by the sheltering concealment?

Whence can an impulse come, even if only an indeterminate one, that alone would convulse the metaphysical age and allow the acknowledgment of the relation to being as unique in dignity?

Impulse and echo.

The convulsing of beings themselves.

The escape attempts into metaphysics.

"Theology" and "anthropology."

"Christianity" and "biologism."

The fraternal seeming-enmity.

Oneness in the same lack of intimation of the persistence in the abandonment of the being of beings.

126. *Being and Time—Being-there*

Being and Time not as title for a treatise but rather as a "domain" that is to be opened, into which the *essence* of the human is to be transformed.

Being-there—what is named thus in *Being and Time* can be set into the thinking word only from out of the experiencing of the more inceptive essence of the truth of beyng.

Freedom as ecstatic steadfastness in the truth of beyng.

Being-there—especially when being-question not fully unfolded, not without passage through the human, but even *when* this is accomplished, and precisely then, steadfastness must be brought into thoughtful reflection.

Correspondence with the philosophy of existence.

127. *"Analysis" and "Analytic of Dasein"*

"Analysis" of the current, *historiographically* present-day "situation" is, in its essence, the metaphysical inversion of the unconditioned synthesis of absolute knowing, which synthesis constitutes the fundamental structure of the "system."

"Analysis" is the making-conscious of each objective presence and of each standard economic political "reality." "Analysis" is only a "function"—that is, a functionary—of this real; it busies itself in a marked trailing-along, without aim or decision. "Analysis" is the implementation of positivism; it must, every time, adjust itself to the situation; it *seems* to direct but is merely pushed around constantly.

"Analysis" is "solution" [*Auflösung*] but is not the release [*Lösung*] of a question; rather, it is the undermining and removal of that which the standard reality can *no longer* admit as real. "Situation-analysis" is the tacked-on interest-calculation in the automatic, which bears the name of the "structural."

"Analytic" (in *Being and Time*) means on the contrary: more originally releasing (destructive) turning back into inceptive projection.

IV. Interpretation and the Poet

A. *Remarks on Interpreting* (Hölderlin-Interpretation) *Cf. Inceptive Thinking* (Cf. Toward Anaximander, Heraclitus, Parmenides [A.H.P.])

128. Interpretation

The saying and the thinking must, in some way, be *accessible*, that is, there must be an impulse toward thoughtful reflection that can emerge from it. This doesn't mean, though, that it should be "*comprehensible*." Were it merely this, it would remain superfluous in advance. What would be communicated by the comprehensible, the understanding of which, without thoughtful reflection and transformation, would be already agreed on, such that it would have already have secured itself and made everything its own in advance?

For accessibility, but against comprehensibility! It is originally in the essential saying itself that both demands become satisfied.

As distinct from a historiographical expounding that is bent on the egoism of the contemporary, and drags the past into the present, conducting itself merely arbitrarily and rapaciously under the guise of objectity, every historical interpretation is a giving.

For interpretation must first ground itself more inceptively from out of itself, surrendering to inception and to history, so that it might emerge more inceptively from its inception.

Whoever, appearing belatedly and inception-less, does not *have the strength for this* giving, shall never venture an interpretation that would be historical, in the sense of historically grounding.

129. The Interpreting

can be taken as historiographical procedure; it then serves explanation and comprehensibility. Comprehensibility is occupied with the *constancy* of the objective. A methodology can then be assigned to this interpreting as the business of historiography. Interpreting then becomes something learnable, and what is learned is to be applied, with appropriate variations, to the most diverse cases. According to the basic positions of historiography, there are various manners and aims of investigation and also, correspondingly, multiple modes of explanation, that is, of historiographical "interpretation."

Such "interpreting" is not trafficked in here; no didactic instructions are to be given; there is absolutely no claim to a "theory" of "construal" [*Interpretation*]. All of this historiographical research is procured most confidently by surveying particular "experiences." Would that its "interpreting" were called (historiographical) *explaining* and the name "interpreting" reserved for another way of thinking. This division of names might be considered arbitrary, but it concerns the matter itself. "Interpreting" cannot be summarily determined just by differentiating the "historiographical" from some sort of "philosophical" interpretation.

Interpreting is given over to inceptive thinking and indeed to the inceptive, which thinks in the other inception and thus must think the confrontation of first and other. First-inceptive thinking is still no interpreting; it is not yet onto-historical.

Interpretive laying-out [*Aus-legen*] is always a laying-forth [*Heraus-legen*] of that which preserves a strangeness in itself, in its *inceptive* (inception-like) essence. This laying-forth brings into the open, but in such a way that it leaves, rather than takes away, the strangeness from the inceptive. This simple *letting* inception unfold-in-itself has the character of a positioning in the far distance [*Weg- und Fernstellung*].

The inceptive is returned into what has been and into what is to come, as into its inner proper domains.

This positioning in the distance distinguishes the interpreting and points to its essential relation to inception.

Such positioning is the saying opening of the in-between, the saying of beyng itself.

Interpreting has in itself the sole essential relation to beyng, that is, to inception, that is, to history.

Onto-historical interpreting is threefold:

1. Interpretation of the history of being (of the first inception and its history, which reveals itself as metaphysics, whereby metaphysics is in itself history,

which is to say the consequential decision of the truth of beings in their beingness).

2. The interpretation of beyng as history, *as* inception. The saying of the incursion of the inter-vening; the word of the event.
3. Interpretation in the consolidation of both these former modes. Interpretation in the *crossing* from first into the other inception. The historicality of this crossing is decided in Hölderlin's word. The preparatory interpretation "of" the poet.

The threefoldness of interpreting springs from the unity of the simple saying of the word of beyng.

What is accomplished in one of the modes also belongs to each of the others.

Thoughtful reflection on interpreting does not serve for setting up a "theory" "of" "interpretation" [*Interpretation*], but only attempts to let the interpreting become more steadfast. Thoughtful reflection is itself interpreting: not interpretation of interpretation but rather self-insertion [*Sicheinlegen*] into its essence.

The interpretation of the history of being, whether it is in the first inception, or in metaphysics, or in the advance saying of the other inception through the poet, soon enters the vicinity of historicizing explanation. Taken from the outside and presented as an attempt to inform, interpretation is no different than explanation—everything can be harnessed into the frame of philosophical-historiographical research. Resistance to this unavoidable misunderstanding leads nowhere. Mere rejection does not make it possible to bring about a steadfastness in beyng. Each must hear the claim of beyng; no one can compel this listening.

Attempts to elucidate the essence of interpretation have only conditional legitimacy. They can awaken the preparedness of the question; they can never bring about steadfastness in the truth of beyng, as this is only eventually appropriated.

In interpreting, there is no "final" interpretation that might, as it were, sublate former positions and gather them into a "correct" result. Every interpretation is inceptive and as such is always the first.

In historiographical explaining, by contrast, the gathering up of results, their working-over and classifying into fixed explanations and comprehensibility, remains always a necessary goal.

Every historiographical interpretation [*Interpretation*] aims at the representation of what the poet, thinker, artist, founder sometime intended and knew as theirs. It will never reach this goal.

Historical interpretation says that which each poet, thinker, artist, and founder already voices beyond [*überstimmt*] and that remains inaccessible. The voicing-beyond protects the attunement of their attuning [*Das Überstimmende gewährt die Stimmung ihres Bestimmens*], whose attuning voice they hear only as an echo, though an echo that lets what is to come sound in advance.

Reckoned historiographically, historical interpretation is always incorrect and arbitrary. But it misunderstands itself, if what it wants is to secure for itself a claim amid historiographical notions.

130. *The Interpreting*

The perennial objection to interpretation, and especially of inceptive thinking, deems that it interprets too much and too uncertainly.

Now—this "too much" remains still too little and too scant, and this "uncertainty" is still not strange enough.

Again and again we make sound human sense into the highest judge and justify this through scientific research of the "exact" rendering of what the text says.

What is the "text"? The fabric of lies of common notions—or the veiling of a simple, singular, uncommon, thoughtful reflection?

131. *Interpretation*

Every thinking and poetizing word, of the singularly few that have been spoken in our history, has the character of being thought and poetized beyond itself. That which each poet and thinker knows never exhausts his word. Its abundance is also not simply a "more," in comparison with what is straightforwardly known from the saying. It is a concealed other, which cannot be immediately "opened up" at once from the straightforwardly comprehensible word. Here once again there is the need for inceptive thinking and poetizing. It is not a matter of the clarity of calculations and of definitions. Still less is it here a matter of the nebulousness of a thoughtless "experiencing." Here there is only the incisiveness of knowledge from out of the unique relation to the uniquely essential, that is, to beyng. From here alone arises an accord, that is, the thinking toward each other of the thinking ones.

132. Interpretation

An interpretation that permits of proof is no interpretation, because to "prove" means a referring of that which is to be explained to what is already clarified and clear. Interpretation, though, leads into the concealed and demands steadfastness in the concealed as the inceptive.

Yet, conversely, unprovability is in itself no evidence for the essentiality of an interpretation.

The test of which is that it itself becomes *superfluous through* that which is to be interpreted.

This *essential* elimination of interpretation alone grounds in such a way that even subsequent and external questions about its correctness no longer have purchase.

Only the interpreted word itself decides the truth of an interpretation, each time, in so far as it is a word "of" beyng.

(Interpretation here never means "historiographical interpretation" [*Interpretation*].)

The truth of an interpretation is decided from out of the essence of truth, with which it is engaged.

The truth of an interpretation [*Auslegung*] never ever first and solely aims at the correctness of historiographical interpretation [*Interpretation*].

133. The "Circle-Structure" of Interpreting

About this, the essential is said for the first time in *Being and Time*, paragraph 152; since it is not enough to have pointed out the circle and to make a few remarks about it in order to make it agreeable. Even Dilthey did not see clearly in this respect, because he was not able to pose the question of the relation of truth and being, knowing so little of the question of being, like all those before him.

In *Being and Time* the circle is positively grounded in the "fore-structure" of being-there. But because the essence of being-there is distinguished by the understanding of being, even this, that is, the relation to beyng itself, must be taken as the approach to an indication of the essential origin of that "structure."

But this relation is eventuated from out of beyng as event. From the steadfastness of being-there, there is no longer any possibility of speaking of "circles" and, over against this, arriving at a secure position, as if it were a matter of a still more hidden "logical" "error."

134. Approach to Interpretation

To rid oneself of the illusion that "positions" gathered together through maximal accumulation might be able to "explain" each other reciprocally and conclusively, when nothing is clarified beforehand, and it is left undetermined from which domain the word speaks and is to be heard.

Instead of which, to take on the arbitrary, along repeated pathways, seemingly from incidental "contemporary" and "personal" meanings, always more projectingly, and projecting further into beyng, returning the word, distinctly, back to itself, and shifting entirely each poem into its proper emphasis.

To differentiate: the truth of an interpretation (historical)

and the accuracy of an explanation (historiographical).

Accuracy *can* be a first directive onto the truth, if it itself arises from a prior glimpse into truth, and that means that it is attuned by the word of what is solely to be said. The essentially historical (arising from beyng as appropriative event) can never be said historiographically—*that* is why all appeals to the present are vain. But the historical, as what is to come, also always seems like a fantastical game or, at best, a singular opinion.

135. Meaningfulness of Poetry
and
Ambiguity of Interpretation

Hölderlin's poetry is meaningful in its saying in such a way that multifarious areas and regions open and close up, are shown and kept secret in the proper domain of saying. This proper meaning of the poem itself (that it is meaningful in itself) holds sealed within it a particular configuration of the truth of poetry. No exposition can make it possible to state this configuration in report or description. Even the poet himself does not know the entire domain of saying; this not-knowing is not the sign of a lack but rather indicates the essentiality of his word, that this is powerful enough in itself to support a genuine history of the opening up of the concealment named by him. The meaningfulness of the poetry must in no way be thought as being the result of a variety of interpretations. On the contrary, that variety is conditioned by the meaningfulness. But not by this alone, and for the most part not at all by this. Ambiguity of interpretation arises from the potential multiplicity of mostly extraneous viewpoints and explanations that are brought to bear on the poetry. Through this there arises a business of interpreting; according to this business, interpreting is in itself poly-valent, eager for different and conflicting explanations, all of which can play out outside the domain of truth of the poetry. Usually the ambiguity of interpretation passes the meaningfulness of the poetry by—; this is in itself singular, demanding the essential word's gathering into one, and withdraws itself from the business of explaining.

The serving of the imageless word, thinking-ahead in thinking—

B. The Poet (Hölderlin) in the Other Inception (Cf. The First Inception) Poetizing and Thinking

136. Thinking-Ahead into the Inception

In all that is inceptive—abyssally going back in moving beyond itself in attunement, having borne all, even the concealed and concealing—it befalls easily, to one who has thought or poetized in its vicinity, that he mistakes what has been already assigned and allotted to him but is not yet held onto as proper domain.

Straying away into the derivative, or into that which in another history is already past, besets every attempt in the inceptive.

Similarly, because he makes his way in the inceptive, he easily becomes obstinately determined that what is past might be the "first," from which every "making possible" might be calculated.

Always this drifts toward a failure to recognize that inception initiates its unfolding in itself, and is thus never fixed like a "starting-point" on which the advancing-away depends and to which it appears to attest and where all that matters is the outcome and the estrangement of inception, insisting on the illusion of possessing what is original. Rarely, thus, is thinking-ahead into the inception already inceptive (i.e., each time unfamiliar).

137. Whither? Thinking and Poetizing

Whither leads the path of onto-historical thinking in its first necessity? To the edge of a chasm, whose precipitous drop opens up as the "end" of metaphysics, and whose bridgeless expanse points across to the summit of the other inception of the grounding of the truth of beyng.

Onto-historical thinking takes over the preparation of the inceptuality of the other inception; it is the leaping off into this. Such thinking prepares a poetizing that, in Hölderlin's hymns, has already taken place, one that unfolds in a genuinely inceptive way. But because this poetry has left metaphysics behind, it is no longer "art." "Aesthetics" has lost all import for the interpretation of this poetry, and every construal of "metaphysical meaning" breaks down.

Whence does it arise, and where does the interpretation of Hölderlin's poetic domain, and the knowledge of its historical inceptuality, have its proper essential inception?[1]

From the knowledge of the history of beyng!

And this knowledge arises from the creative experiencing [*Er-fahrung*] of the overcoming of metaphysics as a historical moment in the history of being (*Being and Time*).

This overcoming *is* itself in the thinking preparation for the response to the claim of beyng.

This claim is opened up as being's abandonment of beings (*Contributions*[2] and *Mindfulness*[3]).

And the abandonment of being appears in the completion of metaphysics as the truth of beings (Nietzsche essay[4]).

Beingness as will to power reveals itself to onto-historical knowledge as machination.

138. *The Holy and Beyng*

Both name the same, and yet not the same.

The names are at one in that they proclaim what holds sway (heals) and unfolds *before* gods and men, before them and beyond them, without, however, being their "cause" and "ground" in any sense of productive conditions. That is also why the determination "absolute" must be denied them. Perhaps every overreaching designation is inadequate (the "highest" and "first"). Therefore, we name them inception, but the inception of the de-cision, in such a way that

---

1. Cf. Inception and Claim.
2. *Beiträge zur Philosophie (vom Ereignis)* (GA 65).
3. *Besinnung* (GA 66).
4. Editor's note: The essay referred to has not thus far been identified.

inception abides as the clearing in-the-midst of the de-cision, as the sustaining in the balance of any assignment of the gods into divinity, of humans into human-ity, of earth and of world to their essential unfolding.

The holy and beyng are, experienced and thought-ahead, names for the other inception. They cannot be displaced back into the history of metaphysics or into the *first* inception (φύσις) that precedes all philo-sophy. The holy and beyng name the most proper history of the other inception.

Because he ultimately encountered inception (calling it, in *"As When on a Holiday . . ."* and for some time after, "nature," and then the "holy," and then generally naming it only indirectly), Hölderlin's word arises from that which, thinking-ahead into the history of being, must be creatively said as appropriative event and thought as the in-between, from whose time-space all beings and their fundamental configuration come to issue. But Hölderlin still does not think this in-between as a developed concept. The intimation of the holy experiences the abandonment of the "earth" by the "world," and the distance of the gods, and the straying of the human. But this abandonment is not recognized as the abandon-ment of beings from beyng, and beyng is not thought as relinquishment, and the relinquishing is not thought as rejection. So, therefore, there lurks around the poetry of Hölderlin's *Hymns* a danger, one that exceeds in an essential way all the usual and nonetheless expected misapplication of his word in everyday ac-counting: that the vaunted words are construed metaphysically and then, with the aid of Rilke's poetry, subsequently situated in a domain in which Hölderlin's poetry is never to be sought, because it has overcome it from the ground up. But because something unusual is sensed, and an unsaid depth intimated, it is easy to believe that one might find help in metaphysics (Schelling—Hegel).—But at the same time it is hasty to think Hölderlin's poetry back into the history of beyng.

139. Toward the Interpretation
of the Hymns

Should this interpretation, which is the creative thinking of beyng in thinking after the poeticized, that is, the holy, remain an error, then Hölderlin, too, would have to be included in metaphysics. Then the other inception, the essential un-folding of beyng itself, would be creatively thought, without preparation, purely from out of incipience. Then the crossing would be still more abyssal, and the end of metaphysics far more capable of lasting, and the intimation of beyng rendered only in the clumsiness of concept.

Should, therefore, the interpretation be an error—what thinking-one would not heed this "should" and hold close to him the constant possibility of an utter straying?

This is above all why, however decisive they might look, there is no presumption of unconditional correctness in this interpretation of the hymns, if ever "correctness" were to be thought of at all, such a thing being unseemly for an interpretation.

140. Hölderlin
The "eternal heart"—"abiding"

Those of the future must experience this as the intimacy of inception in its other inceptuality. And know, thereby, of the inceptive and therefore also concealed relation, inaccessible to historiography, between the "eternal heart" and the ἀτρεμὴς ἦτορ Ἀληθείης εὐκυκλέος that *Parmenides* names. Ἀλήθεια is the essence of φύσις itself.

Yet all this would be too quickly said, if thoughtful reflection were not first directed into the inceptive. All this recollecting lies beyond historiographical comparison, which wants to rush upon evidence.

141. Poet and Thinker

Only inceptive thinkers, not "philosophers" (metaphysicians), stand in essential relation to the poet, though never in the same kind of relation.

We might speculate that thinkers in the first inception had behind them *Homer*, as the one who poetized beyond and ahead of them. And so, for the future thinkers of the other inception, *Hölderlin* would be "the" poet.

Only now, the moment in the history of beyng is different. The playing-out of metaphysics has made the first inception inaccessible, even inverting the being question into the question of value, so that the first-inceptive question of being cannot even be genuinely recalled.

Hölderlin cannot be the thinker that founds-in-advance; he is only ever this when, from out of a more original grounding of the being question as the question of the truth of beyng, thinkers in the other inception *think ahead* to this unique poet, certainly called in advance into the other inception: *think ahead* into the hitherto unprethinkable, first opening time-space to his poetry. Otherwise, his word remains inaudible.

If Hölderlin is the poet of the other inception, then his experiencing of the "truthful" can precisely never be identical with the experiencing of the thinkers who think ahead.

The poet poetizes being; this says that he does not know it, inquire after it and acknowledge it as beyng; rather he names the holy, naming therein the domain of historical decision in its own poetic essence. A thinking can never be extracted from a poetry and reshaped into concepts. But thinking also never arrives at the poetized in its essential word and its proper historicality. Thinking, here, can only become an occasion for bringing a gleaming into the poetry, which must, then, only ever give this out from itself.

142. *Thinking and Poetizing*

When one opines that philosophy must take what it says "from somewhere," one is providing it with a home in "myth," in "religion," in "poetry" and in its own "history." This "obvious" opinion, which instantly knows the advantage of situating "philosophy" in "culture" instead of busying itself with an inessential "philosophy in itself" has, however, lapsed into error before it has begun to opine. This error becomes not less, but only more definitive, with the notion that "culture" itself and its appearances are the expression "of life" and that this expression finds the decisive imprint of its liveliness and actuality in the "political."

Everywhere, "philosophy," in its essence and essential appropriation, has already been *renounced*. The knowledge of the essence of philosophy as the thinking of being has been neglected, though this is a thinking, even if it be only metaphysics, that always arises from being itself and from each historical mode in which the truth of being unfolds.

It is only through beyng that philosophy "is" "philosophy," as the evental appropriation of being into the imageless, knowing word.

(Hereby, the appellation "philosophy" is broadened beyond what is allotted to it in the domain of metaphysics [Plato—Nietzsche].)

Thinking, as the thinking of beyng, has a unique lodging in its belongingness to being, a belongingness that each time eventuates onto-historically as the essential unfolding of being. Thinkers must engage this history within, and it is this alone—whether they are capable of this and how they safeguard it—that decides their thinking essence. Everything else is equally worthless, whether one rests "philosophy," that is, philosophical erudition, on poetry, or on "the political," or on the historiography of philosophy. For sure one might intend to "extract" information, for example, from Kant, about philosophy and its task, or even about its already completed "work." But the escape into any such information-gathering must first have decided whether it now finds and takes hold, in Kant's writings, of that which the thinking of this thinker achieves. To that end, what is needed is a decision about that which is given to this thinking as what is to-be-thought.

This to-be-thought must in turn be revealed in its necessity, and the ground of this necessity and this ground's essence must come to be known. Otherwise, recourse to the information-gathering of philosophical historiography is always just bluff, especially if it is disguised in unassailable names (Plato, Kant, Heraclitus, Hegel). With however much hullabaloo and condemnation of the others the partisanship of one thinker is undertaken, though, it just makes more busy-work for philosophical erudition, which will find itself any slippery path it can to a contemporaneity.

The recourse to the poets is not different from other attempts at making "philosophy" "concrete."

But it might sometime be that, from out of the essence of beyng itself, there might come into the history of beyng a need to recollect a poet, and not just any. If this were to be needful, thinking would beforehand have to have properly reached its inceptuality, in order to first place the word of the poet back into its own essence and so protect it from any misuse by "philosophy." Sometime it might happen that a dialogue between poetizing and thinking might become necessary to the articulation of the word of being. That is, when thinking finds its way back into the essential inception and asks inceptively the question of being, which means having to ask each time more inceptively. That is, if a poet were one day to have spoken just the prologue to the truth of being, because beings had been abandoned by being and the gods had absconded into themselves in their highest being.

Someday it could be that there would be a seriousness in the confrontation of thinking and poetizing; that a thinking might have to think ahead to a poetizing, and therewith this poetizing first might poetize ahead to a thinking, one that risked the most extreme, and therein initiated a saying and a word.

Someday this might be: that historiographical headings such as "philosophy" and "art" would no longer suffice to name that to which a humanity is entrusted, whose determination obligates to the saying of the word of beyng and for which there might once again be a dignity in being and an awe in the human.

143. The Claim of an Interpretation

can never go so "far" as to arrive at an unequivocal certainty about "meaning" because it is not a matter of grasping a "meaning" but of attaining in word the relation to beyng. This says: coming into that preparedness in which the word claims as the word of beyng.

The truth of an interpretation is, then, essential when it prepares the *possibilities* of assignment into beyng. Of course, this possible cannot be the kind of undetermined randomness in which *every* meaning is as good as another. The possible describes unique possibilities that are bound by the necessity of a decision and are thus similarly binding for he who would *hear*, and would not reckon on bypassing all reflecting and thinking. The higher possibilities of the truth of a poetizing and thinking belong to the essence of essential saying that, as the essential, is ever surpassed by its own origins, is inexhaustible, and that all this can itself never properly master. From *this* "content" of a poem emerges the interpretation.

C. Hölderlin-Interpretation

144. Toward the Interpretation of Hölderlin

Each and every poem, every time, is to point into the singular as a telling of the holy.

But never should all the available poems be moved closer together into a breadth of connection with one another that, following the bad habit of historiography, is siphoned off from a basic content, and thus nullified, for the benefit of schools of thought and points of view that are then ascribed to the poet.

Each and every poem says all, and yet none suffices. Because no poem makes possible the apprehension of the immediate, that is, makes the immediate possible.

Nothing that is a being is immediately immediate. But then again, the mediate is itself never immediate, that is, absolutely achieved (as in Hegel's and Schelling's thinking); a *poetry*, though—

It might be, then, that all thinking would transform itself and would no longer think from out of beings.

But then, equally—it would no longer be a matter of mediate and immediate.

145. The "Interpretation"

is no aligning of poetry with present "bustle," which must make everything familiar.

Interpretation demolishes the overgrowth of rash opinions, which take themselves to be the singular measure of truth.

Interpretation represents the desire to understand what is strange. It prepares a readiness to let itself be given over by this strangeness into its concealed truth.

Interpretation forces the all-too-comprehending before their uncomprehending resistance.

146. The Interpretation of Hölderlin's Hymns

must seek to encounter *immediately* that strangeness by which they are affected and, thus, forced to come to the closure of the word.

Only when the interpretation becomes in itself "difficult," and lets the word "appear" seemingly barely comprehensible; only when this difficulty arises from the ease of simple and clear "mastery" of the presentation, is it one that accords with the word, that is, one that is in distant belongingness to it, and guides into listening.

This interpretation *indirectly* has the task of coming to the defense of the poet and his founding for and against the "people."

Hölderlin is that German poet who can never become "popular." A "people's Hölderlin" might at best, perhaps, serve as the creation of a disguise fabricated to protect the unique and concealed from all vulgarity.

All that is common is "vulgar."

It is a good thing that, everywhere, "the qualified" are successfully "at work" on this "people's Hölderlin." And hence no effort need be made to interfere with this bustle or even to expose it in its phoniness. It should remain appropriately undisturbed.

147. The Interpretation as Pledge-Saying

An interpretation is achieved, then, when it has pledged its own word singularly to the poem itself, and has rendered all interpreting—and thereby itself—superfluous.

But, for this pledge, it is necessary to leave to the poetized word a domain of its own, one that creatively unfolds from it.

This pledging relinquishment demands, however, the most strenuous of confrontations.

148. Interpretation
Affirming the Saying and the Telling

To interpret (to expound) the *poetry* does not mean making its essential poly-semy unambiguous and bringing it into a single track but, rather, understand-ing the polysemy in its own legitimacy and configuration; better yet, it means learning to listen fully to the polysemic word and thus sharing in its peculiar inexhaustibility.

Whence arises the restrained polysemy?

Because it is being that is said.

This, however, is the simple.

*

Poetry cannot be figured out from a content and summarized into an account.

Poetry has no "content" at all.

All this in no way says that understanding should be ceded to "feeling"; on the contrary: it is a matter of a knowing.

149. Hölderlin the Poet of Poets

What does it indicate, then, if the (future) poets are founders (bestowing projec-tors of being), that Hölderlin is the poet of poets?

That he himself, in an inceptive sense that thinks far ahead, founds being.

And to say *this* is the will of its essence.

The poet from out of the essence of poetry. Poetry as the word of the holy.

This essence of poetry one-off—not pointing back into the earlier, also not holding up to the future as essential image.

Perhaps the final essence of poetry.

Perhaps the overcoming of all "art."

150. Hölderlin

That Hölderlin's word is still un-experienceable, and that it is still not knowable as the attuning voice of beyng itself—wherein does this lie?

It is that this word prepares the other inception of the history of beyng and that, at the same time, this other inception must be decided beforehand in thinking through the overcoming of metaphysics.

It is because, this time, thinking precedes poetizing. Here, solely and singularly, it is a matter of that of which Hölderlin himself spoke in advance:

"Who has thought the deepest, loves that which is most alive . . ."

(Socrates and Alcibiades III, 16)[5]

But this is the all-living, the holy.

151. Interpretation (the "Circle")

All interpretation moves in a circle.

The recognition of the whole must emerge from the particular and from its securing. But the particular can only be determined and recognized at all through the whole. The one through the other and the other through the one—; this circle, though, only circles out from a center.

It is a matter of leaping into this center—from it alone are the whole and the particular at once knowable in their reciprocal relation.

How, though, and whence the leap into the center? (E.g., of Hölderlin's poetry?)

From out of the thinking that thinks inceptively, and from out of the question of being that, in being asked more inceptively, straightaway stands *beyond* metaphysics.

Thus, thinking makes it possible to know of that which Hölderlin intimated otherwise in advance.

---

5. Hölderlin, *Sämtliche Werke*, vol. 3, *Poems—Empedocles—Philosophical Fragments—Letters* (1798–1800), editing begun by N. von Hellingrath, continued by F. Seebass and L. von Pigenot (Berlin: Propyläen, 1922), 16.

*

Those who can listen are few. None know their number. The number is also un-important. And they do not know one another. Everything is singularly placed on these individuals and on their belongingness to the word.

Whose stillness is the site of its "turning."

Interpretation must encounter the estranging and can only be difficult and like a closing.

Where it turns in stillness toward the inception, there the least thing can surely un-tune everything, and disorder the sounding of the word.

It is difficult to recognize these un-tunings of beyng. And so long as they re-main unrecognized, the stillness of the word is entirely closed up in the unheard. Beings fail and the human is without bread and wine.

> "By the slightest thing,
> A snowflake even, was the bell
> Un-tuned that called
> To the evening meal."
> (*Draft for Kolomb* 4, 2 395)[6]

---

6. Hölderlin, *Sämtliche Werke*, Band 4, *Gedichte* (1800–1806), edited by N. von Hellingrath (Berlin: Propyläen, 1923), 95.

V. The History of Beyng
(Cf. From the History of Beyng 2. Draft, Section 2)[1]

. *Nietzsche* (GA 6.2), 363–416.

152. The History of Beyng

What happens in the history of beyng? With this question we are already positing a difference between the happening and what it is that happens. And in asking about the "what" of the happening, we hunt for a being of beyng. We are already no longer asking about the history of beyng, which beyng itself *is* as history.

The happening of this history is the sole thing that happens "in" it; that is, it happens as itself. So "what" happens? Nothing happens. And this is why the history of beyng is always unknown and inaccessible to historiographical endeavor. Nothing happens. But the nothing is beyng. Nothing happens. The event eventuates.

Ownness *is*. Inception begins and remains in incipience. In-cepting, it takes on the parting and thus delivers the clearing into its simple openness, which has its nonpunctual center in the nothing. Inception eventuates the essence of truth, and thus, looming into and rising out of its own abyss, it is the essential unfolding of beyng itself. Inception is dignity.

What happens in the history of beyng? With this question we are already held up at the difference that differentiates something that has happened from its happening. In asking after what happens, we have in mind a being, even when we name it a "becoming" and attend only to its arising, approaching and decaying. We ask about the beings that pertain to being, and do not ask about the happening in such a way that this alone is itself what happens. If we ask, what happens "in" the history of beyng, then we either do not yet, or no longer, ask about the "history of beyng," the naming of which always indicates that beyng is in itself history. And if we nevertheless adhere to the question in such a form: What happens? Then we come to the answer: nothing happens. "Nothing": no incidents, no facts, no "temporal-historical conditions" into which we like to place "history," deeming it thereby truly grasped in itself. Therefore, the history of beyng is also and remains every time always unknown and inaccessible to historiographical endeavors. Nothing happens in the history of beyng. But the nothing is beyng.

Nothing happens. The event eventuates. The evental appropriation takes on what it at the same time clears as its own: the clearing itself, which is the ownness of beyng. Ownness *is* as inception. Incepting, it takes on what is most proper to it—the parting—and thus delivers the clearing into its own openness, which has its nonpunctual center in the nothing. Inception eventuates the essence of truth, which, because it attunes toward the ground of the true, cannot itself rest on a ground; and from out of this simple plenitude of its essence it has foregone the ground and is, inceptively, abyssal ground.

Thus, inception is the essential unfolding of beyng itself, looming into and rising out of its own abyss. Inception, though, is dignity. Dignity is the simple self-sufficing of inception, to which renunciation and assimilation are denied, as inception is, above all, a concealing and a bestowing and, in that it is beings' essential clearing, is abysmally far from them. Dignity does not effect beings and never furnishes itself with its own justification from effecting. Dignity surpasses all beings and their possibilities, because it allows every being to stand forth in its measure but must also abandon them to sweeping away into the unmeasured.

Rather than something worthy or honored, dignity is the noble itself, whose nobility rests in the uniqueness of inception and nevertheless never shows, as a sign of its status, the rareness alone proper to it. Dignity, in its nobility, is sign-less and is the site of destitution, into whose privation-less holding-sway all repose and every vibrating, all vastness and all nearness, remain enfolded and gathered.

The inceptively reposeful gathering, which does not arise from a togetherness but rather has its essence in-folded into itself from out of inception, is the freeing as which event is eventuated. This freeing is the inceptive essence of freedom. Its essence is concealed in the concealment itself, in which the unconcealment is withheld and the abyssal grounding of inception is covered over in a veil.

The glare of transparency, which appears to lie in all beings as the true being, darkens the simple radiance of inception. Beyng as event has still not eventuated its essential clearing. Beyng remains unknowable and sends into the public realm only the specter of being that, as the abstract, is exposed as contemptible. This is the impenetrable protective wall, for what is without dignity is never capable of infringing on dignity.

153. *The History of Being*

is the essence of history. But in this inceptive (and only inceptive) history, nothing happens; that which has happened is beings. The history of being is event itself, and all that is within it pertains to the event.

It cannot be and should never be described. It is always only a matter of indicating it, in an attempt to prepare for the turning of the human being toward being-there.

The appropriative event, though, eventuates as incipience, and this, in its uttermost in-cepting, is the taking-in-itself of the receding—the concealment into the parting.

Only in the history of being does being safeguard the site of steadfastness, for which inception clears itself.

How, though, should the history of being be experienced? Does this experience not involve the snares of all historiographical reckoning, inasmuch as knowledge is indeed necessary? Or can being itself still be productively thought without all the historiographical padding? Must this not be accomplished when being has a different essential relation to historical humanity? (cf. Summer Semester 1941;[2] *The Guide-Words of Beyng*). Then, historiography can be thrown out by recollecting the holding-sway of being as beingness. In any case all the "thought"-habits of historiography must be given up. The recollective-fore-thinking knowledge of beyng is already the turn into being-there, without this being named as essential.

The history of being (unconcealment, concealment*, the releasing into "appearance" and into non-essence) cannot be brought under a rule. There is no progression here (like some rule, for instance, of three-step "dialectic"). Even if we look over centuries historiographically, we can intimate but little of the historical, because this latter does not consist in a lapse of time but rather holds to its essential site in the event, and that means in the incipience of inception. Incipience itself is the "remaining," in the sense of the ever more inceptive abyssal grounding.

Unconcealment and concealment are not directed from a subject toward a grasping, but rather away from it, and away from the human as *animal rationale* and unfold as incipience; the same goes for "appearance." The holding-sway of the essence, truth.

The event is also no "myth," no "mystery," and no fate, if this is meant historiographically as the original cause of beings, though with the counter-imprint of the in-calculable.

The appropriative eventuation of being-there, and the claiming, still more concealed within it, of the human being into safeguarding the truth of being, is long prepared in stillness. But it also demands from the prepared the great courage of never ever retreating back into beings.

---

* Unconcealment, concealment can be easily mistaken by metaphysics as "appearing" and "veiling" in the sense of Hegel's phenomenology, which conceives everything as the objectivity of the object for a representing by the subject.

2. *Grundbegriffe* (GA 51).

154. Being "Is" Inception and Thus History (History of Beyng)

But being is not the unconditioned, the absolute; neither is it ever conditioned by the human. Conditioning remains alien to being.

But being is the appropriative eventuation into what is proper, such that beings first rise up toward themselves and let themselves be used for its essence.

The appropriative event "creates" and "produces" nothing and does not set about creating beings. The appropriative event eventuates appropriatively.

The evental appropriation raises the nothing-less into truth.

The nothing-less is that which can ever, from out of the appropriative event, be as a being.

Beyng itself, by contrast, is the nothing-like.

Its nothingness is its destitution, and this destitution is the richness of the simplicity of inception.

But what is the advancing-away from being into beingness? What is the history of being as metaphysics?

If being as appropriative event is the evental appropriation of being-there, letting unfold therein the relation to the human, and thus marking out the human being, then must the relation between being and the human not be opened up in the history of being?

But must being itself not surrender itself to this relation and thus to the appearance of having been first established by the human and in human ways?

Is beingness as ἰδέα not the commencement of this unleashing, in which being conceals itself in appearing and shining [Schein und Scheinen]?

And must this unleashing, in accordance with the inceptive essence of being, not also come forth into the most extreme appearance, in which being allows its non-essence to unfold?

Must, though, this unleashing into non-essence in concealment not also be a test of the human being's inceptuality in belonging to the truth of being?

Whether the human might be able simply to be, toward steadfastness in being-there?

But, additionally, must the concealed eventuating not first place the relation of the human to being into direst need, as the human being does not immediately become aware of this relation but, rather, at best, clings onto "beings" and thus onto "beingness"?

Is the history of being as metaphysics, then, not evental appropriation in the form of the testing of the human's capacity for being-there?

And must the plight not be the plight of plightlessness, in order that it become an inceptive [one]?

And is "appearance" not the essential domain of being?

155. The History of Beyng

is not to be revealed to just any "time," because it eventuates the inceptive decision between beyng and beings. Its "time" is always that of an inceptive decisiveness. But precisely because inception is essentially concealment, the furthest advancing-away from inception must yield the impulse for a possible knowing of inception that calls attention to the decision. But the furthest advancing-away is the consummation of metaphysics and is that which, as the instituting of this consummation, throngs yet around the site of metaphysics. This age has its ontohistorical essence in the most extreme abandonment into beings, in the displacement of the human being toward the singular pursuit of beings, in the expulsion of the truth of beings into the forgetfulness of being.

In the history of beyng, this time is the age of abjection.

156. The Abjection of the Age

Abjection is not intended "moralistically." "Morality" itself succumbs to it, along with metaphysics.

Here, abjection means that beyng has surrendered beings to their beingness and displaced humanity from the site of its essence, expelling it into the pursuit of the self-mastery of the human. (Abjection as abandonment, displacement, expulsion.)

For the thinking ones, abjection manifests itself in this: that the powerlessness of the human attacks his essence, and that it is thus that a humanity is no longer able to acknowledge its belongingness to beyng.

All that is known, and whatever is historiographically amassed in thinking and poetizing, is before all else just a matter of the "expression" of a humanity. The "philosophy" of a philosopher is an "expression" of the human, and philosophy disintegrates into psychology, that is, the anthropology of humanity.

The cluelessness of thinking, which has become calculation, no longer knows a limit. But because there only ever belongs to it the reckoning up of need and use, calculation—seemingly "logical"—is incapable of pursuing the essential and of thinking a thought in its decisiveness.

What has already been decided, in consequence of the abjection and its subsequent flight into "psychology," is not even seen:

When everything is "expression" of the human—and this "when" is taken quite seriously—then there is no difference between a word of the poet and the snotty nose of an unwashed urchin or other disjecta of the human body. There is no coming along with "buts" and no escaping into excuses. One must only have the courage for this wisdom, that everything is "expression," then determine the appropriate action.

In the age of abjection, the essence of being is squandered into non-essence and is machination.

In the age of abjection the study of the human becomes the study of the world. Thus trained, the human can no longer glimpse his essence.

In the age of abjection the blind take over the decision as to who may be reckoned as seeing.

In the age of abjection, the abject as onto-historical happen-stance is never recognized. Despite this, metaphysics still must have its formulae. One is extolled for being in possession of a metaphysics of "adventure." "Adventure" is the name for anxiety in the face of thinking.

But because thinking is essentially the allowing of a belongingness to beyng, and because to beyng, as the abyssal ground of inception, belongs the nothing, and because, in the face of the inceptive nothing, thinking is thrown into the attunement of essential anxiety, anxiety in the face of thinking is anxiety in the face of anxiety.

With this anxiety, the pinnacle of cowardice is reached that is at the same time the unknowingness of the essential.

The "metaphysics of adventure" turns into a huge din that would banish abyssal anxiety by establishing an enterprise of forgetting.

Into this din of anxiety-banishment and of forgetfulness-rendering, the word of recollection must place its stillness.

HISTORY AND HISTORIOGRAPHY
(on *"History,"* cf. Fundamental Words;
List of Headings; cf. on History the History
of Beyng, Typescript, pp. 59–69, p. 77[3])

157. The Fissure of the Incepting of the Inceptions

The passage (metaphysics).
The crossing between the first and the other *inception*. (Where does metaphysics belong, here?)
Crossing and receding; receding and its inceptuality.

158. The History of Being and "World"-history

Because being never effects beings, world-history—the incidence of beings—can never be "explained" by the history of being. The question is in error, as if the history of being might be made use of by historians, like the "history of ideas" or something of the sort.

The same errors arise when it is discovered that thinkers and their "philosophy" "only" accompany or follow "incidents" and have no real influence. They in fact have no "influence" of the kind that is meant historiographically. It is an error to expect such, but it is also wrong to be disappointed or, for that matter, pleased by the absence of such connections.

---

3. *Die Geschichte des Seyns* (GA 69), 93, 115.

The "time" of being and of its history is other than the time of historiographical chronology and its epochs. Therefore, the conflict of historians, for example, over the start of modernity, remain necessarily endless; that is, every historiographical explanation is, in its way, "correct." From the possibility of switching these correctnesses issues what one calls the "progress" of science.

159. Being and History

Differentiate: 1. *Historiographical explanation*—regression from a present to a past whereby, in the light of a self-understanding present, this past is itself taken to be what is clear.
2. *World-historical grounding*—how each fundamental position in beings provides the ground for the imprint of beings. (i.e., the Christian God as highest and first actuality)
(e.g., the human as the self-established actor and planner)
3. *Onto-historical appropriation*—here, no "explanation" is possible and every grounding is insufficient. Here, essentially, recollection as the thinking-ahead that prepares steadfastness in being-there.

Note: how immediately (1), (2), and (3) run into and dissimulate one another; how often, toward the first elucidation, the illusory ways (1) and (2) must be traversed, as being-there and steadfastness are "only" inceptive donation.

"*The historiographical*"   is the securely positioned, securable, and explained.

"*The historical*"   cannot be secured, and this, not because knowledge would somehow be unreachable, but because it is in itself nothing securable, is not a being but rather beyng.

Beyng is only creatively thought in thinking, but it is not this creative thinking that first lets beyng stand forth but is, rather, eventual reaching. And it is beyng that allows the creative thinking of history.

"Of history"—but how would we get to it, if we fix it in the "historiographical"?

"Historiography" is human bearing and attitude. "Historiography" always latches on to incidents, because it has secured in advance what is knowable and has done so only in beings.

History is the essential unfolding of beyng and event.

160. History

is the sustaining of the essence of the truth of being. Therefore history is the essential unfolding of being itself. But because unconcealment and concealment belong to truth, there is always, in history, something open, manifest and accessible, that might easily appear to be what is singular and proper to history. The other of history—the concealed, the veiled, the disguised—is then just a matter of the unknown. In "truth," though, concealment is the fundamental trait of history [*Geschichte*]. Reckoned out of what is manifest, the concealed (if ever it is attended to and experienced) appears as the unexpected, that which is sent [*Geschickte*] from out of the incalculable. If it comes up, we make do with accepting this as fate [*Geschick*] and the mode of its appearance as destiny [*Schicksal*].

Why, though, is concealment the fundamental trait of history? Because in it unfolds the incipience of inception, and inception is beyng.

161. History

as specific inception, as decision about the essence of truth.

So, a series of inceptions? This would again be to think historiographically and to see from a standpoint that *seems to be beyond*.

Fissures between inceptions: their looming into the same; nothing in common, rather each time the singular; from each inception the relation to the other ever different; up until now, we stand in the first inception and know hardly anything of the inceptuality of history. Also not a series of fissures; rather, *everything* in every case inceptive.

How an inception ends and goes toward its end, and what this between-"history" is, can also only ever be known from the essential manner of the specific inception; no "*theory of history*," but rather historicity—ours, as way into the inceptuality of the other inception.

162. The Essence of History
(cf. On "Inception")

Neither from out of historiography, nor from the human at all, nor from the happening of beings; rather from out of the truth of beyng. Why so? Because, here, appropriative event, and because, here, the essential inception for the veiled essential unity of what up until now was what was meant by history.

Appropriative event—truth—being-there—grounding of truth.

*

The metaphysical determinations of history:

1. Series of incidents—chronological, cause—effect—*technical.*
2. The constant and its changes—typical of "eternal," spiritual.
3. *Anthropological* conception of history.

*

The rareness of history.

*

The *belongingness* of a humanity into history, ever different and itself *historical.*

*

In the age of the playing-out of the lack of history (abandonment of being), historiography (and in modernity, that means "technique," understood essentially) gains the unconditional upper hand (the "historical balcony").

163. History and Historiography

Why exactly is historiography incapable of establishing a transmittal?

What does transmittal mean? The passing-on of what has gone before, received thus and retained?

Thought thus, the loss of history necessary for transmittal, because in this way any passage into the inceptive is barred.

Transmittal always only calculates, historiographically.

But what if transmittal would be a delivering into inceptuality?

This delivering, though, must eventuate from beyng, and as beyng, and as the essential unfolding of beyng.

Then, and only then, can it itself be taken over but also preserved in an inceptive thinking.

164. History and Historiography (cf. Lecture 37/38 Typescript, p. 40, M.13[4] *on historiographical explanation and historical reflection*; the essential prepared, but not yet achieved and decisively unfolded.)

As soon as one hears, simply following the signification of the words "the happening" [*Geschehen*] (i.e., beyng) in history [*Geschichte*] (whereas in historiography one hears "information"), then the next step has been taken toward an essential differentiation, admittedly only an approximate one, not even preliminary to what decides everything in advance.

From its verbal explication, history [*Geschichte*] might then be thought of as the *object* of historiography [*Historie*], and this object might be allowed to emerge from the objectifying of historiography. Taken this way, if historiographical objectification is taken to its maximum, then it refers not only to past and present but also to the future. This—*even* this—can be calculated historiographically or, at least, positioned into calculability, and from this results a complete historiography: the calculation of the "future" [*Zukunft*] from the "provenance" [*Herkunft*] and the pursuit, established thereby, of the present as passage-through.

---

4. *Grundfragen der Philosophie* (GA 45), 33–35.

Now, with the help of a historiographical reckoning that explores, from out of a present, information about a past, and thereby at the same time calculates the future, one arrives at the future and can now repeat the seemingly profound word that the historical (which is still always and only what is historiographically reckoned and calculated in advance) *is* the futural.

In such ways historiography has become the basic form of knowing (i.e., calculating) beings. Historiography determines the attitude of knowing; it develops into "historicism," whose essence does not consist in emergence within the past but, rather, in the limitlessness of historiographical knowledge, that is, in the complete surrender to *reckoning up*. This can, of course, primarily look backward, leaning on what has gone before, or it can be topical, which means always intent on the "future." Historiography's overgrowth into historicism does not, though, stem from its especially *dominant* position but rather from its being of the same essence as "technique": it is *that* by which historiography is first caught and becomes empowered toward historicism.

History is thereby fully caught in the grip of historiography; it disintegrates into the objectivity of historiography—; is a contrivance of calculation: history is now "made."

The emphasis on the future in the "historical," that is, historiographical, means that this can be given the form of that *through which* the historical might be grasped, whereas the "historiographic" would stick to the past. But this "historical" is also thus conceived purely historiographically. The calculative view of the future, the reckoning of the futural into the present and the attribution of the past to the future are, then, merely the fulfillment of historiography in its unconditionally calculative essence, which can only unfold itself on the ground of "subjectity." (All that is said pertains also to Nietzsche's thoughts on "historiography" and his threefold distinction.)

(The observations in *Contributions* and *Mindfulness* never intend the flaunting of future beings against the past but, rather, intend beyng as appropriative event in the unity of the essential unfolding of time.)

Throughout, nothing is intimated here of history as happening, that is, of beyng. Indeed, the power of historiography is such that it serves to bolster and make definitive the forgetfulness of beyng; for what else is still to be calculated if not the future? Historiography safeguards the ubiquity of knowing.

But "happening": that a being "makes an entrance," that it is given and issues forth; that beings *are*; this is to be known only from beyng; and thence, how it is that beyng allows "happening," and what it is that first actually happens when something "makes an entrance." Then, there has already happened—and *is* happening—that in which any entry of beings eventuates—the truth of beyng, beyng itself as the essential unfolding of truth.

This is the inceptive and proper history—it needs no historiography. Happening is beyng as inception and out of inception.

165. To What Extent "Encounter" Belongs to the Essence of Historical Beings

What does "encounter" mean? That another "truth" approaches that, as other, compels a transformation. But how can "truth" approach?

Steadfastness and intrusion.

Truth—already itself strife of world and earth. This *strife*—the sundering-apart into the opposed, to conjoin the unity of the fully in-between.

The *apparent reticence* toward the encountering—what does this dulling mean?

But "encounter" is often only a form of disguise for a crude objectification of history through an unbridled historiography.

Ages that discover in history only the prefiguring of their own vanity are relieved of the proof that they are merely busying themselves here and there in the swamp of an entirely historicized history and have forfeited even the right to a historical decline [*Untergang*].

Changes in the "historical picture" are only the deformations of historiographical business. These contest their official activities and short-lived "literary" validity out of ignorance that historiography itself is still, in fact, in its essence and essential origin (τέχνη) a progeny of the history of being.

166. History

Past and having-been; passing-by (historiographical) and being; the imperishable *not* as empty sameness—remaining.

The "*imperishable*" usually only the *most transient*, elevated.

The imperishable not such because it *remains* but, rather, because beyond the passing-by of beings and their constancy.

167. The Crossing
(*History* and Inception)

The crossing from first into the other inception.
The first does not lie before, and the other does not stand by ready.
(Crossing as overcoming of metaphysics.)
The crossing must first go back *into* the first (interpretation) and must go forward toward the other.
The singularity of the historicity of this crossing.
Hölderlin and the preparation of the coming.
In the crossing unfolds the gathering of what has been (in its ending) *and* that of what is to come, in preparation.
Ending as the non-inceptuality of inception;
inception is unleashed into its non-essence.

168. History
Inceptuality and Historicity
Decision of the Essence of Truth

History—its *continuity* is determined from the singularity of the inceptive.
 The ever inceptive; *every time* first.
 But the "relationship" of the inceptions?
 Not *historiographical reckoning*!
 And objectifying everything!

169. History

The fissuring of in-ceptions;
the same in the fissuring.

170. History

The once is not yet the *singular* in the sense of what is the essential of an *inception*.

The once belongs to the multiple, through which is stretched the bow of calculation and reckoning from one occasion to another.

The once is the object of historiography.

The singular, though, is the oneness of the sameness of the ever incepting inception.

171. Inception—Advancing-Away— Receding—Crossing

Inception
Advancing-away
Receding   Beginning—end.
Crossing
To experience all inceptively, never as an oppositionally-unfolding [*auseinandergefaltete*] sequence.

VI. *Being and Time* and Inceptive Thinking as the History of Beyng

172. Being and Time

The onto-historical inceptive thinking of that which this title names as inquiry can say the inceptive question as follows:

Being and time are the same.

Being is inception.

Time is inception.

The incipience of inception.

All signs indicate that the age is not ripe to receive the communication of a self-criticism of *Being and Time*[1] (1936); for this "critique" would be "processed" only as welcome confirmation of their suspicions and objections and as a good chance to fall back once more on the relapse of all metaphysics, and as an inducement to be released from every attempt at a leap into the inceptive.

173. Onto-Historical Thinking
and
Absolute Metaphysics

Once the question of the truth of being has first been posed (*Being and Time*) one can, in the usual way of postscripts, easily discover this question "already" in earlier thinkers. Were it discoverable, that is, were it to have "already" been there, then their thinking would no longer be metaphysics. (Note for futile scholarship: it is not a matter of the question of priority, here.)

How is it, though, that one can discover, for example, in and of Hegel, that the question of the truth of being might be being asked?

Here, spirit is absolute being, knowing itself through itself, and this means in its "being" ("actuality"!). One could certainly bear in mind that here, with the absolute, Hegel speaks of "actuality"—a frequently changing essential concept that pertains to ἐνέργεια.

---

1. *Zu eigenen Veröffentlichungen* (GA 82), edited by F.-W. von Herrmann (Frankfurt am Main: Vittorio Klostermann, 2018).

Thus, in a certain way, with absolute being, "being" is known, and this knowledge of certainty is ever the being and the truth of modern metaphysics, which *there*fore has its essential ground in that, as before, the question of being was altogether never posed. How then, ever, that of the *truth* of *beyng*??

174. German Idealism and Onto-Historical Thinking

After the manner of the preceding, it thus appears as if *Being and Time* is caught in the "transcendental" question; the writings immediately following strengthen this impression.

If this status of *Being and Time* is now conceded, a new appearance presses forward. It seems as if the transcending of the transcendental necessarily leads to Hegel and that the thinking of the history of beyng is only a variant of absolute metaphysics.

This would be utterly in error. *Being and Time* holds to the question of possibility only out of necessity. What is essential there, though, is that what is attempted is to think *from out of beyng*.

By contrast, Kant thinks from the object and about objectivity, thinking this from out of the beingness of beings. For Hegel and Schelling all this remains in place, even if turned into the unconditioned.

Hegel never thinks from out of beyng and of its essential unfolding in beings but, rather, from what is most in being and within it (absolute spirit, always only beingness; cf. the "Logic" as metaphysics).

Now, the playing-out of metaphysics (Hegel-Nietzsche) is indeed closest to the crossing into the overcoming. This suggests that the crossing be taken as a variant of the playing-out of metaphysics. One can proceed thus "historically" and bring the state of affairs closer to historically accessible, supposedly familiar fundamental positions. But all this does not hit on the essential.

To call on Hegel for help, in order to make the thinking of the history of beyng "clear," is to want to draw fire from water.

Hegel, furthermore, has never overcome the transcendental but rather first brought out its metaphysical ramifications, because the "conditions of possibility" become purely comprehensible only from out of the unconditioned.

But all *"condition"*[2] is abysmally separated from *appropriative event.*

The *overcoming* of metaphysics is no negation and sublation; in it, the having-been reaches essence and remains, thus, recollected.

175. Being and Time

There should be no misconception, by way of elucidation, that what is now singularly assigned to thinking had, back then, already been known: saying, inceptively, from out of beyng and out of the essential unfolding of its truth.

Only one thing was already clear and fixed at that time: that the way into the truth of being headed toward something unasked and could no longer find support in what came before, as other pathways were to be investigated.

Initially, nonetheless, supports were borrowed from metaphysics, and something like an attempt at overcoming metaphysics through metaphysics was advanced.

What is other is still searched for as metaphysics in the broadest sense of the "being question," although the direction of the question has already leapt over all metaphysics.

The attempt to come at the "existential," and only this, from out of the "existentiell," that is, to think in terms of being and not to be concerned with beings, is an inadequate effort at keeping the being question at once in relation to the human and also in the domain of the question of the "meaning of being" (i.e., of the truth of being).

Nevertheless, if "one" had only had the slightest question about what this "existential" might be, instead of simply swirling everything about in confusion, holding on to the name Kierkegaard like a fetish that makes all questioning superfluous.

This muddle has also now ensured that before all else the historical essence of Kierkegaard remains closed—that historical essence that becomes knowable only when its interpretation refuses to apply as a yardstick the schemata and models of a theology or of philosophers.

---

2. Here as conditioning [*Bedingung*], not event of things [*Ereignis des Dinges*].

In comparison with this, the "pity" about the misunderstanding of "Being and Time" is slight.

176. Being and Time *and Inceptive Thinking*

Being and Time	is a way to the place from which the leap into steadfast thinking can be risked.
Being and Time	is not already this leap itself.
Being and Time	is not even the clearly-knowing preparation of this place.
Being and Time	is an "on-the-way"—that indeed inquires after being, but does not yet know what is even required of thinking.

But the inceptive thinking of being, from the appropriative event of being-there, is equally no reversal of former thinking. Reversals are only entanglements (cf. the Copernican turn).

The other inception—is not mere reversal; rather, it is *inceptuality*, but is thus precisely belongingness into the first inception. First, there must once again be thinkers who think sufficiently simply to be able to think what is the same.

Editor's Afterword

The manuscript *On Inception*, which dates from 1941 and appears here from the literary remains as volume 70 of the *Gesamtausgabe* [Complete Edition], continues the series of great onto-historical treatises that begins with *Contributions to Philosophy* (1938–40).

The manuscript, on the title page of which Heidegger notes, "Summer, 1941," consists of DIN A5 pages, to which a few leaves in DIN A6 format are appended. Besides the manuscript, the editor had at her disposal Fritz Heidegger's typewritten transcript, which consists of 188 consecutively numbered pages. The page numbers of this transcript were noted by Fritz Heidegger usually on the left-hand but occasionally on the right-hand side of the manuscript.

The manuscript comprises six parts (chapters), each with title page, divided partially into subchapters, with a total of 176 sections. All titles of the chapters, subchapters, and sections are Heidegger's own. The roman numerals of the chapters are not in the manuscript but are in the typescript. Chapters 3 and 4 are divided throughout into subchapters, identified in the present volume by capital letters. Because chapters 1 and 5 are not consistently separated into subchapters, their occasional intertitles were not given consecutive capitals. Neither in the manuscript nor in the typescript are the sections numbered. As in the already published onto-historical treatises, though, they are given here throughout in Arabic numerals. Where a section consists of more than one page, an internal section number is found at top right, either in Arabic numerals or with small (occasionally also capital) letters.

For the editing of the volume, the typescript was compared with the manuscript. The paragraph headings were taken up unchanged. One sentence left out of the transcript was incorporated from the manuscript, a few misreadings were corrected, and the punctuation was checked and in several cases added. Heidegger's distinctive and idiosyncratic spelling was adopted but, on the other hand, unusual abbreviations were dispensed with. The abbreviations e.A. for "erste Anfang" (first inception) and a.A for "andere Anfang" (other inception), which occur occasionally, were retained. Underlinings in the typescript, as well as the bold letters in the typescript, are printed in italics.

Six marginal remarks by Heidegger, which come from other copies of the same typescript, are reproduced in footnotes in small Latin letters. References to Heidegger's own writings are added in footnotes with Arabic numerals with particulars of the respective volume of the Complete Edition. References to the writings of other authors were checked and completed bibliographically.

The texts printed on pages 2 and 3 of the volume are already available in slightly different form in *Aus der Erfahrung des Denkens* (GA 13), edited by Hermann Heidegger (Klostermann: Frankfurt-am-Main, 1983), 30–31.

*

The treatise *On Inception* belongs in substance in the vicinity of the *Contributions to Philosophy* and is to be understood, along with the manuscripts *Mindfulness* (1938–39), *The Overcoming of Metaphysics* (1938–39), *The History of Beyng* (1938–40), *The Event* (1941–42), and *The Footbridges of Inception* (1944), as an attempt to open up a new approach to the structure of onto-historical thinking first outlined in the *Contributions*. While the *Contributions* unfold the transition from the "first" into the "other inception" in the belonging-together of six junctures—"The Resonating," "The Interplay," "The Leap," "The Grounding," "The Future Ones," and "The Last God"—*On Inception* thinks the transitional structure of the event in terms of the guiding-concept of "incipience." *Incipience* is Heidegger's word for the ever singular way of the incepting of an inception, for the historical "essential unfolding" of inception in its particular uniqueness. The inceptiveness of inception, however, is nothing that might be located by thinking outside the inception itself. Incipience is no "rule" and no "law" that holds sway "over" inception and outside of it. Incipience is the appropriative event as the particular "fissuring" of the singularity of incepting, the self-differentiating and moving asunder of a historical clearing which, as the inceptive essential unfolding of truth in itself, is at the same time "concealment in the parting." In opening up the transitional place for a reflection on inception, the thinking of incipience is an "intimation" that thinks ahead into the "other inception" in recollection of the "first," into that inceptuality whose essential unfolding is determined from out of the appropriative event that is specifically opened up.

*

I offer heartfelt thanks to the administrator of the literary estate, Dr. Hermann Heidegger, for entrusting me with the task of editing this volume as well as for the review of the prepared text. Likewise, I offer heartfelt thanks to Mrs. Jutta Heidegger for checking the prepared text against the manuscript as well as for the careful reading of the galley proofs. I would particularly like to thank Professor Friedrich-Wilhelm von Hermann for the help in collating the texts and the handwritten notes as well as for the support and advice on all editorial questions. To him, Dr. Hermann Heidegger, and also Dr. Peter von Ruckteschell I extend my warmest thanks for the careful labor of correction.

Freiburg i. Br. Autumn 2004   Paola-Ludovika Coriando

German–English Glossary

der Abschied—parting

der Ab-schied—de-parting

die Abgeschiedenheit—remoteness

die An-eignung—adoption

der Anfang—inception

anfangen—to incept

anfänglich—inceptive

die Anfänglichkeit—the inceptuality

die Anfängnis—incipience

die Armut—destitution

auffangen—to intercept, catch hold of

der Aufgang—emergence

das Aufgehen—the emerging

der Austrag—the sustaining, issuance

der Beginn—start, commencement

die Besinnung—thoughtful reflection

be-stimmen—to attuningly determine.

das Bleiben—the staying

das Da-sein—being-there

die Dazwischenkunft—the coming-into-the-midst, inter-vening

das Eigentum—ownness, proper domain

der Einfall—the incursion

der Ein-fall—happen-stance

die Einzigkeit—singularity

die Entbergung—unconcealment

die Entborgenheit—unconcealedness

die Ent-eignung—dis-appropriation

die Entgängnis—egress

das Er-denken—creative thinking

er-eignen—to eventuate appropriatively

das Er-eignete—the appropriated, eventuated

das Ereignis—event

das Er-eignis—appropriative event

die Ereignung—eventuation

die Er-eignung—evental appropriation

ergründen—to fathom

die Er-widerung—countering-response

die Er-wesung—original unfolding

der Fortgang—advancing-away, progressing

die Fügung—dispensation

das Gemüt—disposition

das Innestehen—standing-within

die Inständigkeit—steadfastness

die Inständigung—steadfast insistence

das Inzwischen—the in-between, in-the-midst

die Irre—the straying

die Sage—the telling

sagenhaft—telling

die Schenkung—donation

seiend—in-being

seynsgeschichtlich—onto-historical

das Sicherwehrens—the self-defending

das Sichfangen—the taking-hold-of itself

die Stimme—the attuning

die Übereignung—the assigning, giving-over

die Überlassung—the relinquishment

der Untergang—the receding

die Verbergung—concealment

die Verschenkung—Bestowal

die Verwerfung—abjection

die Verwüstung—devastation

wesen—to unfold

das Wesen—essence, unfolding

die Wesung—the essential unfolding

die Würde—the dignity

die Würdigung—the acknowledgment

die Zugehörung—the belongingness

die Zulassung—the granting

die Zu-mutung—im-position

English–German Glossary

abjection—die Verwerfung

acknowledgment—die Würdigung

adoption—die An-eignung

advancing-away—der Fortgang

appropriated—das Er-eignete

appropriative event—das Er-eignis

assigning—die Übereignung

attuning—die Stimme

attuningly determine—be-stimmen

being-there—Da-sein

belongingness—die Zugehörung

bestowal—die Verschenkung

coming-into-the-midst, inter-vening—die Dazwischenkunft

concealment—die Verbergung

countering-response—die Er-widerung

creative thinking—das Er-denken

creative unfolding—das Er-wesung

de-parting—der Ab-schied

destitution—die Armut

devastation—die Verwüstung

dignity—die Würde

dis-appropriation—die Ent-eignung

dispensation—die Fügung

disposition—das Gemüt

donation—die Schenkung

egress—die Entgängnis

emergence—der Aufgang

emerging—das Aufgehen

essence—das Wesen

essential unfolding—die Wesung

event—das Ereignis

evental appropriation—die Er-eignung

eventuate appropriatively—er-eignen

fathom—ergründen

giving-over—die Übereignung

granting—die Zulassung

happen-stance—der Ein-fall

im-position—die Zu-mutung

in-being—seiend

in-between, in-the-midst—das Inzwischen

incept, begin—anfangen

incepting—das Anfangen

inception—der Anfang

inceptive—anfänglich

inceptuality—die Anfänglichkeit

incipience—die Anfängnis

incursion—der Einfall

to intercept, catch hold of—auffangen

onto-historical—seynsgeschichtlich

ownness—das Eigentum

parting—der Abschied

progressing—der Fortgang

proper domain—das Eigentum

receding—der Untergang

relinquishment—die Überlassung

remoteness—die Absgeschiedenheit

self-defending—das Sicherwehrens

singularity—die Einzigkeit

standing-within—das Innestehen

start—der Beginn

staying—das Bleiben

steadfast insistence—die Inständigung

steadfastness—die Inständigkeit

straying—die Irre

sustaining, issuance—der Austrag

taking-hold-of-itself—das Sichfangen

telling—die Sage

telling—sagenhaft

thoughtful reflection—die Besinnung

unconcealedness—die Entborgenheit

unconcealment—die Entbergung

to unfold—wesen

unfolding—das Wesen

PETER HANLY teaches philosophy at Boston College and Emerson College. He is the author of *Between Heidegger and Novalis*.

For Indiana University Press

Lesley Bolton, Project Manager/Editor
Brian Carroll, Rights Manager
Gary Dunham, Acquisitions Editor and Director
Anna Francis, Assistant Acquisitions Editor
Brenna Hosman, Production Coordinator
Katie Huggins, Production Manager
Dan Pyle, Online Publishing Manager
Stephen Williams, Marketing and Publicity Manager
Jennifer Witzke, Senior Artist and Book Designer